Work-Based Learning in Cancer and Palliative Care

Other titles available in the Palliative Care series include:

Aspects of Social Work and Palliative Care
Edited by Jonathan Parker

Clinical Supervision for Palliative Care
By Jean Bayliss

Counselling Skills in Palliative Care
By Jean Bayliss

Fundamental Aspects of Palliative Care
By Robert Becker and Richard Gamlin

Hidden Aspects of Palliative Care
Edited by Brian Nyatanga and Maxine Astley-Pepper

Palliative Care for the Child with Malignant Disease
Edited by the West Midlands Paediatric Macmillan Team

Palliative Care for People with Learning Disabilities
Edited by Sue Read

Palliative Care for the Primary Care Team
By Eileen Palmer and John Howarth

Palliative Care in Severe Dementia
Edited by Julian Hughes

Palliative Care for South Asians: Muslims, Hindus and Sikhs
Edited by Rashid Gatrad, Erica Brown and Aziz Sheikh

Policy in End-of-Life Care: Education, ethics, practice and research
By Mary Chiarella

Why is it so difficult to die?
By Brian Nyatanga

Work-based Learning in Cancer and Palliative Care
Edited by Liz Searle and Brian Nyatanga

Series Editor: Brian Nyatanga

Work-Based Learning in Cancer and Palliative Care

edited by
Liz Searle and Brian Nyatanga

foreword by
Professor Karen Cox

QUAY
BOOKS

A division of MA Healthcare Ltd

Quay Books Division, MA Healthcare Ltd, St Jude's Church, Dulwich Road, London
SE24 0PB

British Library Cataloguing-in-Publication Data
A catalogue record is available for this book

© MA Healthcare Limited 2006
ISBN-10 1 85642 235 6 ISBN-13 978 1 85642 235 2

Printed in the UK by Cromwell Press Ltd, Trowbridge, Wiltshire

Contents

Contributors

Maxine Astley-Pepper, Macmillan Lecturer, MNIE, University of Central England

Heather Campbell, Macmillan Lecturer, MNIE, University of Plymouth

Nici Evans, Macmillan Lecturer, MNIE, University of Wales, Cardiff

Suzanne Henwood, Formerly Learning and Development Manager, MNIE, Macmillan Cancer Relief

Nic Hughes, Macmillan Lecturer, MNIE, University of Leeds

Catherine Jack, Macmillan Lecturer, MNIE, University of Leeds

Gail Johnston, Macmillan Lecturer, MNIE, Belfast

Mary Mahoney, Formerly Education Manager, Macmillan Cancer Relief

Eileen Mullard, Macmillan Lecturer, MNIE, University of Leeds

Brian Nyatanga (Editor), Macmillan Lecturer, MNIE, University of Central England

Ann Marie Rice, Macmillan Lecturer, MNIE, University of Glasgow

Megan Rosser, Formerly Macmillan Lecturer, MNIE, King's College London

Liz Searle (Editor), Head of Palliative Care, Sue Ryder Care. Formerly Head of Education, MNIE, Macmillan Cancer Relief

Sheila Small, Macmillan Lecturer, MNIE, King's College London

Claire Taylor, Macmillan Associate Lecturer, MNIE, King's College London

Carole Walford, Formerly Macmillan Lecturer, MNIE, King's College London

Zoe Whale, Macmillan Lecturer, MNIE, University of Wales, Cardiff

Fiona Whyte, Macmillan Lecturer, MNIE, University of Glasgow

Elizabeth Wright, Macmillan Lecturer, MNIE, University of Plymouth

To my daughter Lily, the light of my life, and the one who teaches me most about learning; to my husband Bernard, who is my constant strength and support; and finally to my parents Janet and Ernest and brother Vincent, whose values and humour carry me through. I love you all.
Liz Searle

To Priscilla, Neville, Pamela Lou and Lewin for their love and support always; to my mother for teaching me so much about people; and finally to my closest friends for their encouragement and hours well spent in this life.
Brian Nyatanga

Foreword

This book is interesting and challenging. It brings together a number of individuals from an organization involved in a shared endeavour, to create a virtual institute with the purpose of providing a sense of identity for the members of the organization, as well as education for its workforce. The book tells the story of how the Macmillan National Institute of Education was conceived and its development along the way.

The education of the workforce and the continuing professional development of the current workforce is the business of all organizations. The level, scope, type and nature of education may vary but the essence is the same: education is about encouraging, challenging and broadening horizons at the same time as preparing people to 'do the job'. The institute sought to do this in a way that suited the practitioners it was trying to support, and it is clear from the work presented in this book that the approach adopted was successful.

This book will be of interest to those interested in education, organization development and practice development within healthcare delivery. It sets out how the idea for the institute was developed and made reality. It considers a range of ways in which education can be delivered, in particular work-based learning, and explores some of the challenges that faced those individuals involved in its development along the way. The book describes how new innovations were evaluated and further developed, and in its own way demonstrates how reflective practice can be used to enhance what is being delivered. Finally, the book presents an account of partnership working between organizations – often challenging, often frustrating, but with positive end results. There is much to learn here. I hope you enjoy the process of finding out more.

Karen Cox
Professor in Cancer and Palliative Care
Head of School
School of Nursing
University of Nottingham
Queen's Medical Centre
Nottingham

Acknowledgements

It is hard enough to write for publication as an individual, but even harder to produce a multi-authored text such as this. We recognize that the contributors came from different backgrounds with education as the only common denominator.

Working and learning together enabled a unique experience – a shared vision, which enabled the work depicted here to happen and is highly valued.

Precious time away from families and friends is never easy, but this commitment allowed our story to be told. We hope it will benefit other people beyond the boundaries of cancer and palliative care.

The team extends beyond the contributors to administrative staff, practitioners and people affected by cancer and their families. We are grateful to them all.

Partnerships are essential to the success of any project, and we are indebted to our university partners and Macmillan Cancer Support for their support.

Introduction

Liz Searle

The Macmillan National Institute of Education (MNIE) was set up in 1997. Its purpose was to develop and support the cancer charity's (Macmillan Cancer Support) then 1500 clinical nurse specialists. The vision was to ensure that these nurses had access to tailor-made education and development, with the express wish that this would benefit the care received by people affected by cancer. The public belief was, and still is, that these nurses were experts in their field and in some way the panacea for their problems. At times this brought the nursing workforce into conflict with the organization, as the nurses strived in very difficult situations to bring some form of resolution. This was not the only conflict at this time: further tensions centred on the name Macmillan nurse, which over time had become synonymous with death. The cancer picture was changing and people were living longer, and increasingly there was a need to deliver care at earlier stages in the cancer journey; the name sometimes prohibited this. Today, Macmillan Cancer Support sees a place for care at any point in the cancer journey from diagnosis onwards.

There was an increasing need at this time to support nurses who used their name, and wished to develop their knowledge and skills appropriately; education thus became a valuable and supportive goal. Finally, at this time the organization had completed some work on the strength of the connection that Macmillan nurses had to the organization. This suggested that there was a feeling of detachment, which it was hoped MNIE would address.

A successful conclusion was the survey conducted by Macmillan Cancer Relief in 2003 (Macmillan Postholder Survey). This showed a much stronger attachment to the organization, and education featured highly as something valued by postholders.

Why education?

Education has often been seen as the single most important factor in realizing human growth potential. Today, organizations and businesses have moved from seeing competition as their source of advantage to realizing that the most important contribution an organization can make is its people, its human resource; this realization is well documented (Barney, 1991; Bowman and Ambrosini, 2001; Penrose, 1959; Rumelt, 1984; Wernerfelt, 1984). Resource-based views of the organization see postholders, and particularly specialists, as valuable, rare and someone to imitate and substitute. Public surveys confirmed this view for Macmillan Cancer Relief, as frequently Macmillan nurses were held in high esteem and were the most recognized part of the organization.

Attempting to develop, recruit and retain these nurses, and subsequently allied health professionals, was something for the organization to dedicate some energy towards.

Seven centres of excellence

Initial work on the qualifications and access to education of Macmillan postholders showed, not surprisingly, that access was not equally distributed geographically; there were lots of opportunities around London and the bigger cities. In an attempt to address this, six universities that were geographically disparate across England, Wales and Scotland with Northern Ireland joining later were identified. The criteria for selection were: renowned for cancer/palliative care education; links with the then new cancer centres; and in some cases a history of working with Macmillan Cancer Relief. It took some time for the contracts with these universities to be agreed, but recruitment began to attract the highest calibre educators – two for each unit, plus an administrator. This virtual institute with its seven outreach education units began the work described in this book.

The challenges ahead

One of the fundamental challenges facing MNIE surrounded the idea of the role of a charity. Clearly a large amount of charitable financial resource had been put into this initiative – and clearly charities have a role in adding value, in spending their fund-raised resource well, and in delivering on public expectations and that of the Charity Commission.

A clear goal for all charitable organizations is to add value while not duplicating services, wasting resources, or providing services that should be available to and financed by the public sector. Thus this funding allowing government to avoid its statutory responsibilities.

If the Institute was not to fall foul of these charitable objectives, it needed to find a niche in its provision of education that clearly added value and did not duplicate or subsidize the education sector.

Finding that niche was not difficult. Extensive discussions with Macmillan postholders revealed gaps in the current education provision. There were a large number of specialist degree courses in existence at that time, driven partly by the English National Board specialist agenda and partly by the universities, who saw this specialty as a fast-growing area of income and kudos. In addition, there was a growing body of Project 2000 students completing with their diploma-level qualifications, who were looking for a fast-track route to specialist practice by completing a top-up of a year to a degree; these became available. There were also increasing expectations of existing Macmillan nurses to now be specialists. This constituted a shift in goals when some nurses had joined just to be able to give good nursing care.

The niche therefore lay around practice development, bridging the theory–practice gap, and work-based learning, thus helping both newcomers and existing nurses to become competent specialist practitioners.

This book tells the story of that learning and development journey.

Chapter 1 outlines and defines the notion of work-based learning. It captures the essence of the vision for this education initiative.

Chapter 2 outlines the starting point. Clearly there was a need to understand what were the exact components and competencies of the role of a specialist nurse and subsequently allied health professional. This work started with the development of the profiling tool described in this chapter. From this a series of other programmes and initiatives were developed, including mentorship, role development, 'Setting Out', fellowships, seminars, masterclasses, and a conference programme.

Chapter 3 outlines the role and function of mentorship at specialist level. This programme differs from the more traditional approaches in that it is structured to both support and develop the mentor and mentee and focuses on the relationship and learning contract between the two. This process is supported and developed by MNIE lecturers for a period of one year.

Chapter 4 begins the exploration of role transition from generalist to specialist. This programme focuses on how to negotiate the transition phase successfully and learn from the day-to-day clinical work environment. It bridges between the theory–practice gap. Part of the programme includes the role and development of a practice-based facilitator (PBF). The role of the PBF is to be the guide to achieving a successful transition. Again, this is a 12-month programme.

Chapter 5 explores the need to prepare and initiate effective succession planning. As demands on the healthcare workforce grow, career progression is essential. This chapter highlights how this dynamic process can be managed.

Chapter 6 provides a brief overview of other programmes developed by MNIE. These are outlined here for completeness. Further information can be obtained from the authors of the individual programmes.

Chapter 7 makes a bold attempt to highlight the challenges of the future of work-based learning. It goes on to propose a structured model of continuous professional development, in recognition of the changing nature of the cancer and palliative care health context. This context is also driven by current government policy directives.

Evaluation

As with any education programme, evaluation is essential for monitoring quality, improvement and redesign. All the programmes discussed in this book were evaluated in a systematic way. The profiling tool was evaluated and updated as outlined in *Chapter 2*.

Beyond education programmes

The added value that MNIE brought did not stop at supporting postholders: the Macmillan lecturers were able to contribute to programmes within the universities and also to feed in some of the findings from profiling to curriculum development activities.

The work of the Macmillan lecturer offered a unique role, which was both challenging and exciting. It offered the experience of an interface between education and practice that had not been understood before, and we began to learn what really made a difference to practice and ultimately patient care.

Conclusion

MNIE continues to build on the foundation of adding value and developing the workforce. Its success can be measured by the number of postholders (Postholder Survey, 2003) who now feel a stronger affiliation to Macmillan and the repeated positive evaluations received following the programmes.

Opportunities still exist for the development of new programmes based on the learning of the education team: the role development programme supporting those new to a specialist role and the focus on user involvement are two examples.

This book can be used as a resource, with the reader dipping into chapters at times that are relevant to his/her own learning situation.

As a complete work, here lies the story of organizational development, a journey, a case study of how an education team, given the freedom to grow and innovate, achieved an outcome that benefits both the practitioner and the educator.

We hope that you will gain enormously from reading this book and that the chapters will promote some thinking. We finish the book by offering a reflective model for evaluating the effectiveness of continuing professional development to assist you in planning educational initiatives for the future.

Finally, and more importantly, this book as a whole outlines the journey that one organization Macmillan Cancer Support (formerly Macmillan Cancer Relief) took, in partnership with academic institutions, in paying serious attention to one of its most valuable resources.

References

Ambrosini V, Bowman C (2001) Tacit knowledge: some suggestions for operationalization. *Journal of Management Studies* **38**(6): 811–29

Barney J (1991) Firm resources and sustained competitive advantage. *Journal of Management* **17**(1): 99–120

Penrose ET (1959) *The Theory of the Growth of the Firm*. Blackwell, London

Rumelt R (1984) Towards a strategic theory of the firm. In: Lamb R (ed) *Competitive Strategic Management*. Prentice-Hall, Englewood Cliffs, New Jersey: 556–70

Wernerfelt T (1984) A resource based view of the firm. *Strategic Management Journal* **5** (April/June): 171–80

CHAPTER 1

Work-based learning – same message, new title?

Heather Campbell, Sheila Small

Cynics would say that nurse education has come full circle. The idea that skills-based healthcare occupations are best learned in the workplace has re-emerged as a political issue. However, it is recognized that the relationship between classroom-based continuing professional education (CPE) and performance is still unclear (Brown *et al*, 2002; Department of Health [DH], 1998; Eraut, 1999) and, perhaps more importantly, there is limited evidence of an impact on patient care (Jordan, 2000; Jordan *et al*, 1999). To this end there has been a recent emphasis on creating learning opportunities in and for the needs of the workplace; work-based learning is one of these.

> *'Work-based learning refers to the achievement of planned learning outcomes derived from the experiences of performing a work role or function.'*
> (Glasgow Caledonian University, 2000)

This chapter explores the concept of work-based learning and its influences against a historical backdrop of developments in nurse and healthcare education.

History

> *'Those who cannot remember the past are condemned to repeat it.'*
> (George Santayana, 1905)

Pre-registration

Historically, vocational courses were delivered in further education (FE) establishments as part of a tertiary education system, with an emphasis on preparedness or training for work. Crotty (1993) compared training to education, recognizing that training is associated with a well-defined endpoint, which is achieved by developing clear skills that are often defined by those working within the trade or business. In contrast, higher education institutions (HEIs) had the status – perceived and real – to remain on the periphery, offering education to the few rather than training to the majority.

If training was synonymous with being prepared for the workplace, it applied as much to nursing as to any other occupation. Bradshaw (2001) describes the inception of the nurse apprentice model as emerging with Florence Nightingale and enduring in some shape or form until 1977. Nursing education was delivered by neither FE establishments nor HEIs, but was based in hospital schools of nursing. These were closely aligned with hospitals, student nurses were hospital employees and the syllabus of training was driven by nursing's governing body (Fothergill and Barker) with an emphasis on learning practical skills (Burnard and Chapman, 1990).

During the 1970s, following a review of a new syllabus in 1969, performance in practice in adult pre-registration nursing was demonstrated through verified achievement of tasks and successful completion of four ward-based assessments (Burnard and Chapman, 1990; Watkins, 2000). Although criticized for being task-oriented and ritualistic rather than evidence led, both of these approaches bore some embryonic characteristics of contemporary work-based learning, i.e. self-appraisal, in as much as the learner determined when he/she was ready to be assessed and in part what he/she needed to learn in a particular placement to fulfil the role. In addition, supervision and achievement were monitored by clinical staff and the standard or level of competence was established. While acknowledging that this was a move in the right direction, Burnard and Chapman (1990) argue that this approach did not ameliorate the conflict between learner and service provider and did not exploit the clinical environment as a resource for experiential learning or contribute towards diminishing the theory–practice gap.

As a result, the 1970s slowly saw the beginning of the demise of the apprenticeship model of nurse training. Bradshaw (2001) suggests that this might have been more a reflection of prevailing attitudes and moral values at those times, with a shift from nursing as vocation to the hedonistic culture of the 1960s. However, others recognized the genuine desire for change, indicating the need for a nurse to be responsive to, and more prepared for, a changing healthcare system (Fothergill and Barker) and for disassociation of the role of learner from service provider (Burnard and Chapman, 1990; Dolan, 1993), and an urgency to develop a body of knowledge not structured by doctors (Burnard and Chapman, 1990).

The Briggs Report (Department of Health and Social Security, 1972) made a case for change (Burnard and Chapman, 1990; Macleod-Clark *et al*, 1997), recommending among other things that education should be regarded as a continuing process, that the profession should become more research based, and that institutions of colleges of nursing should be established. However, the report emphasized that while exposure to the clinical environment was important for learning, this should be supported by improved service education collaboration and an emphasis on learning rather than service delivery.

Eventually, in a move to change, a new statutory framework for nursing – the United Kingdom Central Council (UKCC) (established in 1982) and the National Boards (created in 1980) – examined both pre- and post-registration nurse education and stipulated the need for a knowledgeable doer and links with higher education (www.nhshistory.net/nursing.htm pp 1–9). This resulted from the Briggs proposals and the Nurses, Midwives and Health Visitors Act 1979. In 1986 the UKCC published its proposals for nurse education, and Project 2000 'A new preparation for practice' was launched in 1989.

The perceived implications, among many health professionals, were that it would result in a move away from the medical model, with a focus on the holistic nature of man and a health rather than disease orientation. The clinical: theory ratio was to be 50:50, but with exposure to traditional nursing placements occurring much later. Assessment would be around defined competencies (Project 2000), and their achievement would be enabled and supported by student supernumerary status and a well-prepared mentorship system.

However, Project 2000 was not without its critics. Quite obviously, it did not remedy the attrition rate, as there was still a nursing shortage (Edmond, 2001). In addition, findings from the Peach Report *Fitness for Practice* (UKCC, 1999) indicated that there was evidence that newly qualified Project 2000 staff were not fit for practice, often being ill prepared to take on their concomitant post-qualifying responsibilities (Gilmour, 1999; Luker *et al*, 1999; UKCC, 1999), which raised doubts about this academic drift.

Although research subjects in an evaluation study undertaken by Macleod-Clark *et al* in 1997 considered that the pendulum had swung too far towards theory at the expense of practice, other findings indicated that despite a deficit in Project 2000 diplomates' initial management ability, the development of such skills was responsive to a post-qualifying, supportive environment. And despite a common belief that diplomates lacked preparation in practice skills, these were perceived as initial skills deficits only.

Although these evaluation findings were relatively positive, following the Peach Report recommendations (UKCC, 1999) the focus was a move to competency-based education and a re-introduction of practice skills early in the programme (Watkins, 2000). Despite this approach already sounding rather familiar, the new model of competence-based nurse education was rolled out as a pilot in 2000 and provided the standard for pre-registration nurse education. This was further revised by the Nursing and Midwifery Council (NMC) in 2004 with the introduction of the NMC standards of proficiency, which provide the framework for pre-registration programmes, stipulating the outcomes to be achieved for progression to the branch programme and competencies for entry to the register.

It would be cynical to suggest that this re-emphasis on practice skills early on in the programme and competencies (a key feature of many vocational courses and work-based learning) was a knee-jerk reaction to the recruitment and retention crisis of nurses within the NHS. With healthcare needs rather than professional evolution once again dictating the format of nurse education, presenting the argument in this way may have seemed the natural order. However, without long-term evaluation of the impact of Project 2000 a real insight could not be afforded, and the prevailing judgment at that time may have eventually been seen as ill founded.

Post-registration education

'All wish for knowledge but no one wishes to pay the price of it.'
(Juvenal)

'The specific purpose of CPD and lifelong learning is to equip nurses to develop expert skills and knowledge to support their insights into patient need, service development and health improvement.'
(Royal College of Nursing [RCN], 2002)

Initially, in the 1970s, post-registration education was determined by a range of clinically oriented courses integrating theory and practice under the auspices of the Joint Board of Clinical Nursing Studies in England and Wales and of similar boards in Scotland and Northern Ireland. This responsibility was then taken on by the four National Boards.

These programmes of study were unaccredited, and for many trained nurses at that time a curriculum vitae (CV) would present an eclectic profile, which often reflected knowledge and skills deficits in a specific area, or expediency to meet a work-related demand, rather than a coherent approach to developing a career pathway. In Scotland, however, the picture was somewhat different, with a recognized qualification in professional development.

Healthcare professionals today have a duty to keep knowledge and skills up to date (UKCC, 1994). The requirement has gradually gathered momentum, endorsed not only by a political/statutory framework (*The NHS Plan* [DH, 2000]; *Working Together, Learning Together* [DH, 2001]; the skills escalator [DH, 2002]) but also by the recognition that pre-registration education is not a once-and-for-all preparation (Macleod-Clark *et al*, 1997) and that nursing – like medicine – requires a clear career pathway. The relationship between higher education and the NHS therefore remains a buoyant market economy, but with the drive firmly in the hands of service again, with both purchasers and providers working towards preparing practitioners who are fit for practice (UKCC, 1999) at pre- and post-registration levels.

Higher education providers in England have attempted to contribute to continuing professional development (CPD) by developing accredited academic pathways at diploma and degree level for nurses pre- and post-Project 2000, which offer common core modules and area-specific modules. The advantage of this is that practitioners can develop an appropriate portfolio to meet job or personal requirements (Chalmers *et al*, 2001; Chapman and Howkins, 2003). For the specialist nurse, the UKCC collaborated closely with HEIs to develop the Specialist Practitioner Award. In Northern Ireland, Scotland and Wales there is a firm commitment to an all-graduate nursing profession at the point of registration (RCN, 2002), which would reflect the existing status of other professions allied to health.

However, academic programmes are expensive and releasing the workforce for undergraduate and postgraduate study would present a challenge to maintaining care while developing the workforce (Chapman and Howkins, 2003). It might also be argued that highly educating the tip of the iceberg of the workforce might not be the best use of money, and that it might be better to distribute education opportunity across all bands of the healthcare and nursing workforce.

The NHS Plan (DH, 2000) demonstrated a commitment to increasing the numbers of staff in health care, recognizing that there is a growing emphasis on changing the way in which services are delivered and questioning the accepted boundaries of professional roles. New nursing roles are emerging in response to the changing needs of health care. Often these roles develop at a faster pace than professional and statutory frameworks, sometimes without any clear consensus regarding the appropriate education for these roles. This may leave nurses in a vulnerable position, and there is a growing need to support those nurses in role transition and to identify and articulate the learning required to enable them to conduct the role.

The *Agenda for Change* proposal (DH, 2004) has taken some steps to providing that structure: while recommending a minimum educational framework for preparation for roles, it conceded that this could be achieved through formal education or equivalent for most levels. In order to meet the aforementioned challenges, the RCN (2002) is convinced that clinically based scholarships, work-based learning and e-learning are the way forward for maintaining the CPD momentum.

Work-based learning

'Knowledge is of no value unless you put it into practice.'
(Anton Chekhov)

As has been described, the focus on the partnership between higher education and healthcare providers is relatively new. However, changes in healthcare policy have been matched by developments in educational policy. The Dearing Report (1997) called for education to be more responsive to the skills and knowledge required by employers of their workforce. In addition, HEIs have been encouraged to widen participation and improve recruitment and retention by creating more flexible pathways.

Work-based learning has much in common with a number of approaches to adult learning, and is based on the principle of experiential learning (Kolb, 1984) and problem-based learning (Burnard, 1991; Evans, 1994). An expanded definition of work-based learning is provided by the Glasgow Caledonian University (2000):

> *'Work-based learning is a subset of work-place learning. It refers specifically to the achievement of planned learning outcomes derived from the experience of performing a work role or function. In addition, it is normal practice to complement the experiential learning with directed reading, research or group work to ensure that learning is placed in the context of current theory or practice. Such experiential learning must be capable of being evidenced and assessed before it can be recognised by the university.'*

There is a distinction between workplace learning and work-based learning. Workplace learning is a generic term for the learning that is normally provided by the employing organization. This is linked with the notion of training and is normally delivered by the employing authority. It may consist of short-term activities which emphasize practical skills that are immediately applicable to the job, such as manual handling training, basic life support and general health and safety issues.

Boud *et al* (2001) describe work-based learning as providing a framework to enable the value of experiential learning to be made explicit and accredited. Its special work-linked features enable learning to take place at, through and centred on the working environment. These aforementioned descriptions capture some of the key features of work-based learning:

- It is learning that is planned and not ad hoc.
- What has been learned needs to be demonstrated and acknowledged.
- It is experiential.
- It is relevant to a work or role.
- The learner is an active participant in the process and should instigate the boundaries for learning.
- It is flexible and can be applied to most learning environments.

Burnard and Chapman (1990) clarify the key components of experiential learning as involving the learner in action, encouraging reflection on his/her experience, clarifying and analysing that which has been learned and applying it to new situations. They also point out that the activities of both experiential and work-based learning reflect an adult learning approach.

The work-based learning approach is enabled by delivering programmes of study over a longer period of time; these are designed to enable the student, mainly through self-directed learning, to acquire the relevant knowledge and skills to fulfil a specific role or project within his/her workplace. Work-based learning encourages the learner to identify what he/she requires to learn in his/her practice area. This may be articulated through the provision of specific learning outcomes or competencies, but should reflect each individual's requirements. By its very nature, therefore, it is an individualized approach.

How learning is to be achieved and demonstrated needs to be clearly defined. Evidence of achievement in formal accredited work-based learning is a key component and is often expressed through a learning contract.

As can be seen, reflection on workplace activities is another element of this approach to learning; in addition to this, however, the student must have the opportunity to develop practice within a context of contemporary theory and research:

> *'A work-based learning philosophy supports the idea that theory can be effectively assimilated if it is meaningfully related to well-researched practice.'*
> (Birchenhall, 1999)

7

This is supported by Jarvis (2000) who postulates that, when explaining the theory–practice gap, what is highlighted is the changing nature of practice situations, which challenges the learner to apply knowledge and learn in and from practice.

There is also a key responsibility to provide identified support and mentorship for students in both the clinical setting and the HEI. The availability of effective mentorship is also essential to the effectiveness of the learning environment (see *Chapter 3* for further information on mentorship).

Birchenhall (1999) attributes the growing popularity of work-based learning to its potential to capture the essence of workplace activity.

The advantages of work-based learning are linked to its ability to create and provide learning that is responsive, flexible and relevant to current healthcare needs. In addition, the approach has the potential to deliver skills in critical thinking, synthesis of theory, reflective practice, practice development and the management of change (Clarke and Copeland, 2003; Flanagan *et al*, 2000). These advantages are impressive; however, the success of this approach will depend upon a shared commitment and dual responsibility between educational institutions and healthcare providers. This requires an understanding of the approach as well as a shared vision and development of working practices to facilitate collaborative working. There need to be formal arrangements and collaboration between educational institutions and healthcare providers. This aspect of shared responsibility for planning and creating the learning process is the key to the effective implementation of work-based learning (Birchenhall, 1999; Boud *et al*, 2001)

So, is work-based learning a new phenomenon? It can be seen from the historical overview that much of nursing preparation has emphasized being prepared for the workplace, taking place in the workplace. However, in its efforts to do this it has not exemplified an adult learning approach. The processes of the training model met service requirements through achievement of predetermined knowledge and skills (Burnard and Chapman, 1990), with little room for negotiation. On the other hand, Project 2000 exemplified a more lateral, radical approach, but one that may inadvertently have contributed to increasing the theory–practice gap. Both of these trends have been mirrored in post-registration CPD.

Work-based learning has sought to apply adult learning principles to prepare nurses to utilize and transfer the appropriate knowledge and skills to a variety of situations. By so doing, they are meeting service need while endeavouring to limit the theory–practice gap. It could be argued that this is either the cheap option or a pragmatic way of responding to the changing face of nursing and healthcare provision.

References

Birchenhall P (1999) Developing a work-based learning philosophy. *Nurse Educ Today* **19**(3): 173–4

Boud D, Solomon N, Symes C (2001) New practices for new times. In: Boud D, Solomon N (eds) *Work-based Learning: A new higher education?* SRHE/Open University Press, Buckingham: 18–33

Bradshaw A (2001) The Nurse Apprentice 1860–1977: *The history of medicine in context.* Ashgate Publishing, Aldershot

Brown CA, Belfield CR, Field SJ (2002) Cost effectiveness of continuing professional development in health care: a critical review of the evidence. *BMJ* **324**(7338): 652–5

Burnard P (1991) *Experiential Learning in Action.* Avebury, Aldershot

Burnard P, Chapman C (1990) *Nurse Education: The way forward.* Scutari Press, London

Chalmers H, Swallow V, Miller J (2001) Accredited work-based learning: an approach for collaboration between higher education and practice. *Nurse Educ Today* **21**(8): 597–606

Chapman L, Howkins E (2003) Work-based learning: making a difference in practice. *Nurs Stand* **17**(34): 39–42

Clarke DJ, Copeland L (2003) Developing nursing practice through work-based learning. *Nurse Education in Practice* **3**(4): 1–9

Crotty M (1993) The influence of educational theory on the development of nurse training to education in the United Kingdom. *J Adv Nurs* **18**(10): 1645–50

Dearing R (1997) *Higher Education in the Learning Society.* Report of the National Committee of Inquiry into Higher Education. HMSO, London

Department of Health (1998) *A Review of Continuing Professional Development in Practice: A report by the Chief Medical Officer.* HMSO, London

Department of Health (2000) *The NHS Plan.* HMSO, London

Department of Health (2001) *Working Together, Learning Together: A framework for lifelong learning for the NHS.* HMSO, London

Department of Health (2002) Pillar Two – ensuring the NHS provides a model career: The skills escalator. In: *HR in the NHS Plan: More staff working differently.* DH, London

Department of Health (2004) *The NHS Job Evaluation Handbook.* 2nd edn. HMSO, London

Department of Health and Social Security (1972) *Report of the Committee on Nursing.* (Cmnd 5115) (Briggs Report). HMSO, London

Dolan B (ed) (1993) Reflection and celebration. In: *Project 2000: Reflection and Celebration.* Scutari Press, London

Edmond C (2001) A new paradigm for practice education. *Nurse Educ Today* **21**(4): 251–9

Eraut M (1999) *Developing Professional Knowledge and Competence.* 4th edn. Falmer Press, London

Evans N (1994) *Experiential Learning for All.* Cassell, London

Flanagan J, Baldwin S, Clarke D (2000) Work-based learning as a means of developing and assessing nurse competence. *J Clin Nurs* **9**(3): 360–8

Fothergill and Barker http://www.mhhe.heacademy.ac.uk/resources/nursing.asp pp 1–5 (accessed 20.01.06)

Gilmour A (1999) *Report of the Analysis of the Literature Evaluating Pre-registration Nursing and Midwifery Education in the United Kingdom.* Commissioned by the UKCC. UKCC, London

Glasgow Caledonian University (2000) *Good Practices in Work-based Learning.* Department of Learning and Educational Development, Glasgow

Jarvis P (2000) The practitioner-researcher in nursing. *Nurse Educ Today* **20**(1): 30–5, discussion 36–44

Jordan S (2000) Educational input and patient outcomes: exploring the gap. *J Adv Nurs* **31**(2): 461–71

Jordan S, Coleman M, Hughes D (1999) Assessing educational effectiveness: the impact of a specialist course on the delivery of care. *J Adv Nurs* **30**(4): 796–807

Kolb DA (1984) *Experiential Learning: Experience as the source of learning and development.* Prentice Hall, New Jersey

Luker K, Carlisle C, Riley E, Stillwell J, Davies C, Wilson R (1999) *Fitness for Purpose.* Report to the Department of Health. The University of Liverpool, Warwick

Macleod-Clark J, Maben J, Jones, K (1997) Project 2000. Perception of the philosophy and practice of nursing: preparation for practice. *J Adv Nurs* **26**(2): 246–56

NMC (2004) *Standards of Proficiency for Pre-Registration Nursing Education.* NMC, London

RCN (2002) *Quality Education for Quality Care: A position statement for nursing education.* RCN, London

Santayana G (1905) *The Life of Reason: Reason in Common Sense.* Scribner's, New York; Constable, London: 284

UKCC (1986) *Project 2000: A new preparation for practice.* UKCC, London

UKCC (1994) *The Future of Professional Practice: The Council's standards for education and practice following registration.* UKCC, London

UKCC (1999) *Fitness for Practice.* The UKCC Commission for Nursing and Midwifery Education. Chair: Sir Leonard Peach. UKCC, London

Watkins M (2000) Competency for nursing practice. *J Clin Nurs* **9**(3): 338–46

CHAPTER 2

Identifying the learning and development needs of specialist practitioners in cancer and palliative care

Zoe Whale, Mary Mahoney, Nic Hughes, Carole Walford

Education and training remain a central element in enabling individuals to adapt and shape the changes required for them to be effective at work in the 21st century. This is even more important when providing care to patients suffering from life-shortening conditions. In order for healthcare professionals to deliver effective care, it is paramount that they have adequate educational support and development.

The quest for better understanding of the development needs of clinical nurse specialists (CNSs) was a primary driver for the development of a National Institute of Education, supported by Macmillan Cancer Relief. The inception of this Institute – the Macmillan National Institute of Education (MNIE) – in 1998, as a UK-wide initiative, enabled the identification of learning needs, collated through educational profiling, to be translated into a range of programmes for educational support and development. It was equally important that such an initiative addressed the needs, not only of the individual, but also of the profession and the employing organizations.

This chapter will:

- discuss the development and implementation of a systematic tool to elicit the development needs of CNSs and, later, other allied health professionals (AHPs)
- discuss the profiling process aimed at creating an individualized development action plan
- report the findings of evaluations and reviews undertaken of profiling.

Specialist practice

The Calman–Hine report (1995) endorsed the importance of the availability of CNSs in cancer and palliative care service delivery. Webber (1997) explored the evolving role of the CNS, while Bousfield (1997) investigated how CNSs think and experience the role. Around the same time the professional and regulatory bodies were developing guidelines for specialists (Royal College of Nursing [RCN] Cancer Nursing Society, 1996; United Kingdom Central Council for Nursing, Midwifery and Health Visiting [UKCC], 1997).

The directives from the UKCC (1997) were the first specific requirement for training to take place in order to register as a specialist practitioner. In many areas of practice, including cancer and palliative care, learning to become a specialist had happened 'on the job', with no formalized training. To enable a better understanding of what 'the job' was, MNIE developed a tool to collect these data.

Developing the profiling tool – principles

At the outset the education team developing the tool agreed that the underpinning values and principles guiding the work would be:

- To develop a tool that would enable CNSs to learn how to learn in order to increase their efficiency and effectiveness. This in turn might increase job satisfaction and reduce stress and potential burnout syndrome, thereby enhancing retention of specialist practitioners.
- Learning needs are best identified in a partnership relationship between the CNS and the manager of the service, facilitated by the lecturer.
- Learning needs are best met when learning styles of both the specialist and anyone supporting the specialist are known and used to shape and support the learning and development experiences. Awareness of preferred learning style is essential in selecting the appropriate learning experience.
- Learning opportunities can be identified, utilized and supported in the workplace.
- Supporting learning is the key to ensuring that development will continue.
- Core competencies for functioning at specialist level are included and utilized as part of the tool.

Development of an instrument for educational profiling

There were three main phases of the development process: design, development and piloting.

Designing the tool

A mixed group of nursing professionals and stakeholders (CNSs, CNS teams, managers, Macmillan Cancer Relief personnel, regional nurses, chief executives and representatives from the UKCC, English National Board [ENB] and RCN) who had an interest, or had made a significant investment, in Macmillan CNSs self-selected to participate in the work. Interviews and focus groups took place over several months in late 1996 and early 1997 to explore perceptions and to ascertain the dimensions of the CNS role. Within the data collected, patterns were identified which were congruent with current literature on the structure and function of the CNS role, and which formed the basis for a new model of specialist practice (*Figure 2.1*). This model became the foundation for developing the profiling tool.

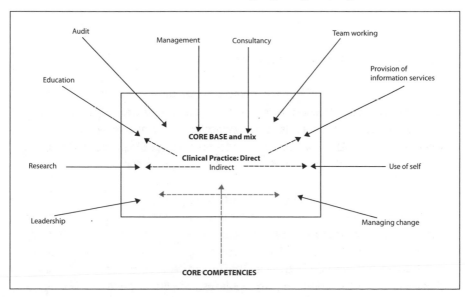

Figure 2.1: Diagram showing the relationship of the components of the Macmillan nurse specialist role to one another. Context: the delivery of palliative care in a variety of settings, interacting with different patient groups.

The model suggested that all the components of the role were interlinked and interdependent in the daily context of work. This concept of the role ensures, for example, that the activity of research does not become separate from the activity of clinical practice: rather, that the knowledge, skill and expertise associated with one component informs the practice of the others and vice versa. This clearly demonstrates that a CNS is not a researcher or educator who separates the components into specialist activities, but rather a practitioner who integrates these components into his/her daily work. This appears to be borne out in the work of Hamric and Spross (1989) on primary criteria for CNS practice. Most CNSs work across a multiplicity of settings and will always need to work flexibly as change agents, encompassing all components in their daily work.

The profiling tool consisted of the following:

- learning styles questionnaire (Honey and Mumford, 1986)
- record of previous education and work experience
- self-rating questionnaire outlining the components and competencies of the CNS role (*Box 2.1*)
- individual SWOT (Strengths, Weaknesses, Opportunities, Threats) analysis
- education/development action plan.

Box 2.1: Components and competencies of the CNS role

The use of self in practice
Demonstrates an awareness of self and is able to develop self as a positive influencing factor in practice. Is able to critically analyse and reflect on practice, work within boundaries, and is able to identify and utilize appropriate support structures, eg. clinical supervision.

Leading and developing practice
Challenges professional and organizational boundaries in the interest of patients, and to improve health outcomes. Is able to develop and apply strategies to learn effectively from others. Demonstrates ability to work collaboratively across the disciplines and, where appropriate, take the lead in developing documentation, standards, policies and clinical guidelines. Networks locally, regionally and nationally to develop collaborative working with other healthcare professionals. Acts as a resource for staff, patients and carers.

Providing effective health care (direct and indirect services)

Uses a confident and assertive approach, demonstrates ability to identify and manage complex care episodes. Is able to lead and empower other healthcare professionals using appropriate referral and discharge policies. Delegates to other professionals, utilizes resources effectively, and is able to work within a multidisciplinary team setting.

Evaluation and research

Seeks opportunities to apply new knowledge and promotes the use of evidence-based practice. Is able to access and utilize research material and seeks opportunities to broaden and deepen nursing knowledge. Always chooses interventions based on sound rationale. Is aware of the importance of continually auditing and evaluating own and others' practice using a broad range of valid and reliable methods. Is able to utilize the results of audit to inform and improve practice.

Develop self and others

Continues to address his/her own personal and professional development needs. Develops and uses appropriate strategies and opportunities to share knowledge and expertise with other professionals, patients and carers. Continually strives to improve practice through teaching and educational activities.

Improving quality and health outcomes

Operates efficiently and effectively within a culture of clinical and cost effectiveness (clinical governance). Is able to utilize information systems and has an understanding of how information technology can contribute to clinical practice. Demonstrates decision-making skills and ability to balance the conflicting components of the role. Takes the lead in the implementation of health and social policy and utilizes a variety of information systems. Seeks opportunities to influence health policy locally, regionally and nationally. Actively promotes the service.

Working across professional and organizational boundaries

Demonstrates ability to work flexibly across professional boundaries. Is aware of the potential macro and micro issues that can influence team dynamics. Is able to manage group and organizational relationships in a way that supports intended outcomes.

cont../.

Innovation and changing practice

Is proactive in managing and promoting change to improve practice and health outcomes. Takes the lead in the implementation of local and national standards as appropriate. Is able to contribute to the development of his/her area of practice, and think laterally about his/her own and others' practice in order to generate new solutions to meet the needs of patients and carers.

Developing and piloting the profiling tool

The tool was then tested to frame an educational development plan for individuals, giving some CNSs a structured learning plan for their role for the first time in their career. The tool was piloted in late 1997 to ensure that it was 'fit for purpose' and to test the effectiveness of the process. At this time the UKCC was constructing a framework for 'higher level practice', including descriptors (UKCC, 1997), which gave both organizations the opportunity to work collaboratively, sharing ideas about the way forward for specialist/higher level working.

Three objectives were tested within the pilot. These were:

- to develop an understanding of how to gain maximum benefit from the system of profiling
- to clarify how these roles could work more effectively together (Macmillan lecturer, newly appointed CNS and manager)
- to gain feedback from the facilitator and the CNS about the experience of using the profiling tool.

The pilot sample originally included 20 CNSs and their managers. Briefing materials were sent to them, and to a number of Macmillan personnel and other stakeholders involved in the work, for communication purposes.

The conclusions from the pilot were:

- Two to three hours were needed to complete the profiling exercise.
- Approximately one additional hour was needed to meet with the CNS's manager.
- Two and half hours were needed, on average, to produce a draft report and action plan for review and modification by the CNS.

- Supporting documentation needed further development.
- Competencies for each component of the role required further development in order to make them more specific.

Early feedback from those profiled indicated that most practitioners felt that:

- It was useful having a written record.
- They became more confident in what they were doing and where they were going educationally.
- They became more aware of learning styles and more understanding of how this influenced their work.
- Working relationships with managers improved.
- Clarifying the CNS role boundaries and expectations was as an extremely positive outcome.
- The process was a supportive platform for further work.
- Profiling needed to be a one-to-one confidential exercise.

Early feedback from the managers included:

- The facilitator needed to understand the role.
- There was the potential for reducing education spend by focusing on the individual's identified development needs.
- The plan gave equal value to learning opportunities available within the organization and to external educational programmes.
- Profiling helped to assess the needs of the CNSs more broadly than previously.
- The exercise was simple and straightforward to carry out.

Towards the end of 1997, an additional pilot on the profiling tool was conducted with 800 experienced Macmillan nurses. The evaluation from this further pilot clearly demonstrated that the tool was useful. Comments included:

"To review the job, reflect, reinforce, refresh and re-evaluate the CNS role in light of current developments has been really helpful."

"Excellent to review competencies and reassuring/empowering to know that the right road is being taken."

"Very difficult, heavy subject, but really important to bash out – find a consensus/clarity about what direction."

"How great it was to have this time focused on personal practice – going back to work recharged."

"I feel much more confident now to articulate the difference between a generalist and a specialist."

"Having the tool there to explore and a personal plan to take away felt really valuable."

Establishing the process

Rolling out the profiling tool

In September 1998 the MNIE lecturers were introduced to the profiling tool. It was a new concept and process, one that the ten lecturers grappled with within a workshop format. There was an air of excitement at the prospect of building a bridge between the practice setting and assessment of education needs. The focus was clear from the outset – that education profiling was development in its broadest sense, not solely formal education in terms of academic accreditation, but also encompassing assessment of lifelong learning, personal development needs and a skills-based approach to the CNS role.

A flexible approach was agreed in order to facilitate the profiling process across Macmillan education unit (MEU) regions with unique demographic characteristics. The resulting profiling standard (*Box 2.2*) provided a framework for contact with NHS managers, Macmillan service development managers and Macmillan CNSs. It outlined the expected turnround time from initial profiling interview to a first draft going to the CNS, and then the subsequent review meeting with the CNS. The development of the standard took time as there were many regional differences; yet there was also a commitment from the lecturers – a commitment to equity of provision for CNSs, be they based in the far north of Scotland, the peninsula of south west England or in central London. The varied distances that the lecturers would travel to undertake the exercise resulted in further consensus that some review meetings could be undertaken by telephone, but that the initial interview should be face to face.

Box 2.2: MNIE Profiling Standard

Standard Statement:All Macmillan postholders (excluding medics) will be offered educational profiling in order to facilitate their learning and development.

S = Standard statement for MEU structure
P = Standard statements for MEU processes
O = Standard statements for MEU outcomes

SI   Regional MEU checklist completed

PI   MEU will send pre-meeting information to postholder and manager at least 3 weeks before profiling meeting
P2   MEU lecturer will make contact with the postholder's manager prior to profiling
P3   MEU will request copies of postholder's CV, operational policy, job description and completed profiling tool to arrive before the profiling meeting
P4   Lecturer and postholder will review above documents before profiling meeting
P5   Lecturer will discuss consent and keep signed consent form
P6   Profiling tool will be used as a framework for discussion
P7   Draft action plan sent to postholder
P8   MEU will receive signed action plan (signed by postholder and manager)
P9   Non-receipt of action plan followed up by MEU
PI0 Review (about 12 months after profiling) will be offered to postholder
PII Action plans will be stored in accordance with the Data Protection Act

---

OI   All Macmillan postholders (excluding medics) will be offered educational profiling
O2   MEUs will have signed consent forms for all those postholders who have been profiled
O3   All Macmillan postholders will have a signed action plan following the profiling exercise
O4   Applications for Macmillan Cancer Relief education grants from postholders who have been profiled will be accompanied by their action plan

MEU = Macmillan Education Unit; MNIE = Macmillan National Institute of Education

---

Geographical and regional differences were challenging, but it was agreed that the need to link with the CNSs face to face in their workplace would override the cost in time and travel. It was agreed that the main target group for the process would be CNSs who had been in post less than one year. Relationships were established with the Macmillan service development manager teams and the lecturers built links within their Macmillan region.

Delivering the outcomes

The first challenge was gaining access to each new CNS. The Macmillan service development managers were asked to copy the new appointment form for each new CNS to the local MEU. This was then to trigger an introductory letter from the MEU offering the CNS the opportunity to be profiled. The MEU lecturers in turn divided up the geography of the patch. The patches were determined from the Macmillan Cancer Relief regions and varied greatly in the number of postholders; distances between the MEU and CNSs in the north of Scotland or south west England were not comparable to proximity of CNSs in the south east. However, traffic jams and the effect of the city rush hour meant that travel times were comparable.

Travel was not the only challenge, as lecturers brought their previous work experiences to the process. Facilitation styles varied and each lecturer developed his/her own style for the process, with some taking 2 hours to complete the initial interview while others found it hard to contain it within 4 hours. The process was a new and intense listening exercise, which meant that some lecturers managed two profile meetings in a day while others felt that they could only do justice to one. The writing-up process also took time to learn. The individual CNSs were asked to proofread the document and to modify the text before a final copy was agreed by both parties. The investment of this amount of time and energy was substantiated by the positive feedback received as the process was subsequently reviewed and evaluated.

Findings from the profiling process informed the first programmes developed by MNIE. Initial programmes included 'Setting Out', a workshop for new postholders that introduced the CNS role, a re-working of the established weekend seminars to give a clearer education focus, and consideration of the need for a mentorship training programme. The monitoring of profiling raised healthy debate among the lecturers. It was acknowledged that the process should be delivered in a similar manner in each Macmillan region. There were also valid concerns regarding the contents of the document and the lecturer's ability to form reasoned judgment on the clinical competence of the CNS. It was agreed that profiling was a subjective tool – one on which the lecturer records, at face value, that which the CNS chooses to disclose.

In 2000, the profiling exercise was opened up to postholders who had been in post for more than a year. As a result, several MEUs profiled all CNSs in their region. In other regions the waiting lists continue to grow. Profiling has never been compulsory and the demand across the Macmillan Cancer Relief regions is linked directly to the concentration of posts and attrition rates.

In 2000, MNIE expanded to appoint two lecturers at the University of Wales College of Medicine. In preparation for this sixth MEU, a further internal review of profiling highlighted the need to develop a guide to using the document. A subgroup from MNIE wrote a briefing document (*Appendix 1*), which was given to the new team in Wales and also subsequently to the MEU lecturer appointed to the MEU in Northern Ireland in 2001. Changes in MNIE lecturers at the original five sites also brought the opportunity to look at the process with fresh eyes and pose challenges to the now-familiar tool. By the end of 2001 the tool was in use with CNSs across four nations.

Informal feedback showed that the profiling exercise was highly valued by CNS postholders. Consequently, other Macmillan specialists asked to be included. The ensuing debate regarding the profiling of AHPs resulted in further amendments to the process. MNIE decided to undertake a pilot using the profiling tool with five AHPs from each region and then look at its usefulness to this group. It was hypothesized that the tool was generic, yet MNIE lecturers were aware that it was developed for use with CNSs. The findings were that the core content of the document focused on professional and educational development and was easily transferable to other disciplines. The challenge to the lecturers (who at that time were all from a nursing background) was their knowledge of the opportunities available to AHPs. Many AHPs were already of graduate status, whereas there were still some CNSs who needed to complete degree-level study as a core part of their development needs. Informal feedback from the AHPs as to the value they placed on profiling led to the process being opened up to Macmillan AHPs in 2002.

The development of other programmes within MNIE and the varied demands across the country for profiling led to ongoing developments being considered:

- The debate as to the value of the components of the role section within the tool continued.
- It was agreed within MNIE that the whole profiling process was valued by the participants and should still be undertaken; however, participants would be asked if they would prefer a summary document.
- The challenges of distance and demands on lecturers' time resulted in further changes being made in 2002, when a pilot was started to use the

tool in one region as a personal development tool – sending it via email and discussing it with the postholder via the telephone subsequent to his/her completion of the emailed version.
- In another region, one of the options offered is completion of a reflective account of the profiling meeting and submission of this as a summary to the MEU lecturer as a record of their meeting (instead of the typed document).
- In a region that has been constantly inundated with profiling requests, a group of experienced CNSs has been trained to undertake the process; the evaluation will be undertaken by a Master's thesis supervised within the local MEU.
- The outcomes and findings of the profiling process across the UK, Scotland and Wales would be evaluated through a research project overseen by MNIE (Astin *et al*, 2006).

The initial concept of profiling was that it was not a static process with a defined end, but that it mirrored its underpinning principle of lifelong learning. It has held its place as a valued process with both the lecturing team and participants in the process. The lecturers have been flexible in their approach but have not lost sight of the fact that the process is simply an opportunity to facilitate the participant's reflection upon his/her learning to date and the opportunities that he/she may benefit from in the next 12–18 months. The confidential nature of the one-to-one discussion is still central to the process, thus allowing honesty from the CNSs and AHPs. The CNSs and AHPs indicate the value of the process by asking for reviews and repeats as they change posts; in response, the MNIE lecturers continue to develop fresh approaches in order to offer the essence of profiling in a format that is in line with the demands of higher education and clinical practice today. It also enables MNIE lecturers to identify needs for course and seminar development.

Creating a climate of evaluation and review

Why evaluate and review?

Evaluation can be described as determining the value or worth of, to appraise (*The Cassell Concise English Dictionary*, 1997) an intervention, policy, service or innovation. The term 'evaluation' is used in a number of contexts and may be employed to describe a number of diverse activities, ranging from a formal, systematic examination of a planned intervention, to the informal subjective assessments that colleagues make in the course of their everyday work. The aim of MNIE is to create a climate of development and learning, hence a culture of both informal and formal evaluation becomes crucial in guiding educational developments in areas where there are few precedents. This climate of informal review leads to many questions being posed (and not always answered), many heated debates and a need to make consensus decisions in order to move forward with educational interventions.

There are a number of overwhelming reasons why profiling in particular should continue to be open to review, evaluation and critical discussion:

- Profiling is labour intensive and therefore a costly way to deliver educational support.
- There is a need to demonstrate the effectiveness of profiling in terms of professional development of CNSs and AHPs and impact on patient care and services.
- Quality monitoring: there emerged a need to monitor whether the original aims and values of profiling were being upheld and operationalized.
- There is a poor evidence-base for the effectiveness of appraisal tools for healthcare professionals.
- Macmillan Cancer Relief needs to ensure that educational profiling remains relevant within the context of a rapidly developing healthcare system, particularly in the field of cancer and palliative care.
- As other Macmillan professionals (eg. information radiographers) seek individual educational support from Macmillan Cancer Relief, there is a need to explore the relevance of the profiling tool to other posts.

An interesting debate was ongoing within MNIE about *which* aspects of profiling to evaluate and *whose* perspective to consider. There appeared to be subtle differences in the way that lecturers interpreted the purpose of profiling, eg. in terms of the degree to which profiling is related to competency for specialist practice. In addition, anecdotal reports from lecturers identified that profiling can produce a 'ripple effect' on the Macmillan team, the multidisciplinary team and indeed the whole service. This effect was seen as positive by some (but not all) of the people involved.

Groundwork: principles of evaluation

An internal review of the evaluation literature was undertaken, and from this work some guiding principles of evaluation of MNIE's activities (including profiling) were agreed. These included:

■ Key stakeholders should be identified and incorporated into any evaluation.
■ The aims, objectives and outcomes of profiling should support the overall aims and direction of Macmillan Cancer Relief.
■ Evaluation of profiling should include structure, process and outcome indicators.
■ Efforts should be made to use existing validated tools for evaluation, but in the absence of a suitable tool a new tool should be developed.
■ The impact of profiling on patient care and services should be evaluated.

These principles have been continually helpful in directing the various phases of profiling evaluation and 'selling' the evaluation process to busy colleagues.

Further discussions on profiling among the stakeholders generated a formidable list of those who may have a pertinent view on the processes and outcomes of profiling. This list included Macmillan CNSs, other Macmillan professionals, patient groups cared for by Macmillan professionals, the NHS colleagues and employers of Macmillan professionals (including team members, line managers, lead managers and trust boards), the lecturers undertaking profiling, Macmillan service development managers, and the associated education, service, policy and fundraising departments at Macmillan Cancer Relief. It was acknowledged, therefore, that evaluation and review should necessarily be phased and ongoing in order to meaningfully access the views of others.

Educational profiling has been evaluated in three ways. The perspectives of Macmillan CNSs and MNIE lecturers have been ascertained, and a wider consultation, which included Macmillan service development managers, cancer leads across the UK and the Department of Policy and Planning at Macmillan Cancer Relief, has been conducted. These are reported below.

Evaluation of profiling from a practitioner perspective

In 2001, a major evaluation of profiling was undertaken from the perspective of Macmillan CNSs who had been profiled in England and Scotland between 1 April 1999 and 31 March 2000 (345 Macmillan CNSs in total). At this time, profiling was not available to Macmillan CNSs in Wales and Northern Ireland, although there were plans to offer profiling on a UK-wide basis.

In the absence of a suitable evaluation tool, a tool was developed with the help of an external consultant and was piloted and adapted, first on 17 CNSs and subsequently on 50 CNSs. The Macmillan CNSs who had been profiled during the specified time were sent the final questionnaire by post with a covering letter. The questionnaire covered demographic details (including how long the respondent had been in post), usefulness of the components of the profiling tool and usefulness of the profiling process. 'Usefulness' responses were invited on a five-point Likert scale: 'not at all'/'a little'/'moderately'/'quite a bit'/'a great deal'.

Open questions about the impact that the profile had on personal, professional and educational development were also included. The respondents were also specifically asked 'Has the profiling exercise made any difference to patient care?' and asked to give examples. A total of 265 questionnaires were returned (77% response rate).

The findings from this evaluation were as follows:

- The majority of the CNSs (85%) scored the usefulness of the profile components as 'quite a bit' or 'a great deal'.
- 197 CNSs (74%) were very positive about the usefulness of developing an action plan.
- Those in post for less than one year or longer than 3 years returned the highest scores in terms of usefulness of exploring the context and components of their post.
- Just over half the respondents (54%) responded positively to the open question 'Has profiling made any difference to your personal development?' Forty-three per cent responded positively to the question 'Has profiling made a difference to your professional development?' The responses related to gaining confidence, giving focus and direction to their development, expanding awareness and activity, and highlighting strengths.
- A further category of positive responses identified by the respondents was feeling 'supported' and 'valued'. This support made CNSs more confident in seeking support within their own organization.

- 128 CNSs (48%) were able to identify differences that profiling had made to their educational development. These included the pursuit of a wide variety of educational courses and identification of workplace activities to meet learning needs.

Comments made in the open question section of the questionnaire included:

"Greater insight into my strengths and weaknesses offered direction and guidance in my personal development."

"I have felt affirmed in what I have considered as personal development, and challenged in others, which is a good combination."

"I had just started studying for a degree as I was profiled. The profiling exercise enabled me to choose modules from the degree that are relevant to my role, i.e. challenging practice, clinical leadership, collaboration."

"There were a number of problems in our service, which I knew needed addressing. Profiling gave me the confidence to articulate these and to develop a plan of action."

"Turned threat into opportunity."

"Helped me in gaining managerial support."

"It was amazing to have 3 hours dedicated to oneself. It made me re-evaluate my role, skills and competencies."

"It is excellent to have someone from outside the trust and it is wise of Macmillan to combine this with educational grants."

Impact of profiling on patient care

Ninety-two CNSs (35%) were able to identify differences that profiling had made to patient care. These included indirect impact through empowerment, reflective practice, confidence and education of others. Direct impact on patient care covered a wide range of practice issues relating to changes in assessment methods, information giving and development of systems and services to improve standards of care, for example:

- development of a formal assessment and referral pathway for people with colorectal cancer
- development of user-friendly information
- improvement of care pathway to reduce the wait for radiotherapy
- development of alliance with tissue viability team and contribution to a change in wound care policy
- greater skill to act as a patient advocate
- development of a nurse-led telephone clinic
- development of communication skills
- assessment of patients for depression
- assessment of sexuality in patients with haematological cancers
- participation in the strategic planning of breast cancer services.

It is important to note that the lecturer helps the CNS to meet any practice goals by identifying the personal development needs required to fulfil his/her aims, and discussing a variety of ways in which these development needs may be met. The discussion of practice goals is a key reason why the involvement and support of the line manager is crucial to the viability of the resulting action plan.

A minority of responses related to difficulties with the profiling process, including the intense time pressures that some CNSs were under, which compromised their ability to engage with profiling and consider their own development needs (3; 1.1%). A very small number of CNSs also said that the profiling had not made any difference to the plans they already had in place (6; 2.3%) or they felt that their organization was not supportive of their professional development (2; 0.75%).

This formal feedback from CNSs was extremely useful in augmenting the subjective views of the MNIE lecturers undertaking the profiling, who sometimes described ways in which profiling had transformed someone's working life. The results of the evaluation showed that profiling is generally viewed very positively in terms of helping CNSs in their personal, professional and educational development. The supportive nature of the profiling process also emerged as a valuable facet of profiling.

On the basis of this feedback, MNIE resolved to continue to offer profiling to Macmillan CNSs, to extend the profiling process to AHPs and to review the profiling tool to ensure multidisciplinary utility in a changing NHS climate.

Evaluation of profiling from the MNIE lecturer perspective

An internal review of the profiling tool and the process of profiling was undertaken in 2002 from the perspective of the 15 MNIE lecturers who undertook profiling. The lecturers were asked their views on the profiling information, the profiling tool, the follow-up and review meeting, documentation of the profile, travel arrangements and contact with managers.

The responses demonstrated continued support for the concept of profiling and the underpinning values. In accordance with the comments from CNSs, there was support for reviewing the profiling information and the profiling tool. However, the lecturers identified that travelling could be burdensome, especially when follow-ups and reviews were added to the main profiling consultation. The lecturers also identified wide variations in the degree to which managers came forward to be informed and be involved in the process. The agreed recommendations from this exercise were as follows:

- The profiling tool, information and standard should be updated to reflect changes in the postholder population, changes in health policy, the views of CNSs and AHPs and changes in the data protection laws.
- CNSs and AHPs should be made aware of the explicit links between profiling and Macmillan Cancer Relief educational grant applications.
- MNIE lecturers should continue to contact managers and send profiling information to them when a CNS or AHP came forward for profiling. A meeting or telephone appointment should be offered and a record kept of the response to this invitation.
- Preparation work should be done before the profile by lecturers, CNSs and AHPs in terms of reviewing curriculum vitae (CV), job description, operational policy and reflection on components of the specialist role.
- The learning styles questionnaire should be applied in accordance with lecturer and CNS or AHP preference.
- Follow-up appointments and review meetings continued to be seen as important, but these meetings could involve face-to-face, email or telephone contact to improve efficiency.
- CNSs and AHPs should choose the format of the written profile, i.e. a summary report, or a full report of the profiling meeting.

Review of the profiling tool and wider consultation

By 2002, CNSs and AHPs across the four countries of the UK were being offered profiling. Informal feedback from managers and other disciplines (including medicine) suggested that the profiling tool, although developed from a nursing model of specialist practice, appeared to have utility for any clinical post that featured a transition from a generalist to a specialist role in health care. For this reason a working group within MNIE was established to review profiling in the light of current healthcare policy and practice. Some key national documents (listed in *Appendix 2*) were reviewed to inform this exercise.

Common themes emerged from these documents around:

* competency, skill acquisition, advanced decision-making and knowledge for practice
* multidisciplinary and multi-agency teamworking
* continuing professional development, work-based learning, appraisal and creating a learning environment
* promoting evidence-based practice, quality monitoring and evaluation
* leadership and management development, which included innovations in healthcare delivery and integrating user involvement in every level of health care.

Based on this review, modifications to the profiling tool were proposed by MNIE, and a consultation exercise was undertaken in 2003 with Macmillan service development managers, cancer network lead nurses in England, cancer leads in Wales, Scotland and Northern Ireland, the Macmillan Professional Reference Group and the Department of Policy and Planning at Macmillan Cancer Relief (82 people).

The consultation feedback incorporated broad support for the modified profiling tool and its utility within the current climate of health care. Multidisciplinary applicability was felt to be improved, although there was some discussion about the discipline background of the lecturers (all nurses by background). The emphasis on core skills and role evaluation was welcomed. A number of interesting comments were made as to how the tool could be further developed for a different purpose, eg. to augment the quality assurance process, or for utilization as a performance appraisal/competency tool.

By 2004, profiling utilizing the modified profiling tool (*Box 2.3*) was offered across the UK to all Macmillan CNSs, AHPs and information consultants.

Box 2.3: Modified educational profiling tool

Background
(Context of the post, education and learning history, work history)

Components of the specialist role

Providing effective health care
(MNIE lecturer explores the degree to which the CNS/AHP/information consultant...)
Analyses and reflects on own practice, is effective as an independent practitioner, has advanced decision-making skills, uses self to influence practice, utilizes effective communication skills, manages complex care episodes, demonstrates user-focused practice, is effective within multidisciplinary team, positively impacts on other teams, develops effective information strategies, demonstrates sound rationale for clinical interventions, empowers non-specialist staff, balances caseload with other components of role, works effectively across professional and organizational boundaries.

Develops self and others
(MNIE lecturer explores the degree to which the CNS/AHP/information consultant...)
Demonstrates continuing professional development through work-based learning and other mechanisms, takes opportunities to develop practice through teaching and educational activities, demonstrates user involvement in educational activities, demonstrates self-awareness about the impact of his/her own development on colleagues and the service.

Quality, evaluation and research
(MNIE lecturer explores the degree to which the CNS/AHP/information consultant...)
Demonstrates quality improvement initiatives, improves health outcomes of client group, demonstrates ability to work with information systems, data handling and IT, audits/evaluates care and services, works within the context of clinical and cost effectiveness, demonstrates user involvement in quality improvement, evaluation and research, able to access research evidence, able to analyse/utilize/disseminate research evidence, participates in research initiatives.

Leading and developing practice
(MNIE lecturer explores the degree to which the CNS/AHP/information consultant...)
Demonstrates resource and people management, demonstrates user involvement in service and strategic development, works strategically in the context of national policy and local service development, positively utilizes and influences political agenda, utilizes leadership and consultancy skills, networks locally, regionally and nationally, generates innovative work practices/extended roles, implements local and national standards, manages change, demonstrates project management skills.

Current strengths

Learning and development needs

Opportunities and constraints to meeting needs ´

Proposed ways of meeting needs (action plan)

Future developments in educational profiling

A period of implementation of the modified profiling tool and processes needs to be completed before further evaluation and review. Future activity will evolve from informal feedback from postholders and their managers. Additional impetus to review may come from the findings of a study commissioned by MNIE to ascertain, from the profiling information, a view of the collective education and development needs of Macmillan CNSs, and to identify the most common opportunities and barriers facing them (Astin *et al*, 2006). This study found that the development and maintenance of specialist knowledge and expertise to enable Macmillan CNSs to function as specialist practitioners were key education and development needs. Teaching and dissemination skills were also documented as requiring development.

There were more 'constraints' to education and development cited than 'opportunities'. Sources of support, funding and education were the top-ranking 'opportunities' cited. Resource constraints, clinical commitment and workload, and balancing competing demands were the top-ranking 'constraints' to education and development cited.

Future reviews of the educational profiling tool may be influenced by a more performance-driven, competency-based climate and further evolution of the role and work demands of specialist practitioners. Changes in the delivery of specialist health care will also be influential. Active discussion is ongoing about how an objective assessment of the impact of profiling on patient care could be carried out.

In addition, other performance review tools may be available and being implemented in health care, which will require Macmillan Cancer Relief to scrutinize the 'added value' of the profiling tool. There will also be a continual need to appraise cost-effectiveness and there is likely to be greater exploration of the applicability of the tool, and of the process, to NHS staff working in other specialisms outside cancer and palliative care.

Conclusion

The current Macmillan Cancer Relief educational profiling tool represents nearly a decade of development, implementation and evaluation and, through continued positive feedback, remains a core service provided by the MNIE. Profiling has generated unique information about the background, experiences and learning/development needs of Macmillan postholders, which enables Macmillan Cancer Relief to inform programmes of education and support. A climate of evaluation and review is now thriving because of the rich information gleaned from profiling. This enables the profiling process to contribute to the commitment of Macmillan Cancer Relief to offer appropriate support to health professionals irrespective of their discipline, remit, organization or geographical location. Although complex and time consuming, the profile exercise highlighted, among other things, areas of support needed for Macmillan practitioners. As a result of this development, programmes including mentorship (*Chapter 3*), role transition (*Chapter 4*), and 'Setting Out' (*Chapter 6*) were developed by MNIE and offered to all Macmillan practitioners.

References

Astin F, Closs S J, Hughes N (2006) *The Education and Development Needs of Macmillan Clinical Nurse Specialists: An analysis of educational profile archives.* Report to Macmillan Cancer Relief, London. Unpublished

Bousfield C (1997) A phenomenological investigation into the role of the clinical nurse specialist. *J Adv Nurs* **25:** 245–6

Calman–Hine report (1995) *A Policy Framework for Commissioning Cancer Services. A report by the Expert Advisory Group on Cancer to the Chief Medical Officers of England and Wales.* HMSO, London

The Cassell Concise English Dictionary (1997) Special new edition. Edited by Kirkpatrick EM. Cassell, London

English National Board (ENB) (1997) *Specialist Practitioner Programmes and Transitional Arrangements for the Use of the Specialist Practitioner Title.* ENB, London

Hamric AB, Spross JA (eds) (1989) *The Clinical Nurse Specialist in Theory and Practice.* 2nd edn. WB Saunders, Philadephia

Honey P, Mumford A (1986) *The Manual of Learning Styles.* 2nd edn. Peter Honey Publications, Maidenhead, Berks

RCN Cancer Nursing Society (1996) *Guidelines for Good Practice in Cancer Nursing Education.* RCN, London

UKCC (1997) *PREP – Specialist Practice. Consideration of issues relating to embracing nurse practitioners and clinical nurse specialists within the specialist practice framework.* UKCC, London

Webber J (1997) *The Evolving Role of the Macmillan Nurse.* Macmillan Cancer Relief, London

CHAPTER 3

Mentorship – a key to developing the workforce

Megan Rosser, Ann Marie Rice

This chapter considers the concept of mentorship in relation to facilitating work-based learning and development. The origins and growth of mentorship are explored, along with its application to health care. A specific mentorship training programme offered by the Macmillan National Institute of Education (MNIE) is described and the value of this programme is demonstrated through comments obtained during an evaluation of the programme.

Defining the concept of mentorship

The origins of mentorship

Most authors acknowledge that the earliest act of mentoring is described in Greek mythology, when Odysseus entrusted his son to the older, wiser Mentor in his absence. There appears to be academic dispute as to whether the true supportive role of Mentor is made explicit by Homer in *The Odyssey*, or in later French writings about the adventures of Telemachus, son of King Ulysses (Roberts, 1999). Whatever the authorship, it is acknowledged that Mentor, and at times the goddess Athene, in Odysseus' absence provided the qualities of counsellor, teacher, nurturer, protector, adviser and role model to Telemachus through many of life's transitions.

Since Homer's writing, it has come to be accepted that the term 'mentor' means a wise and trusted adviser. This interpretation has influenced contemporary, shared understanding that mentorship involves the guidance of a trusted, wise, experienced person to enhance the personal and professional development of a less experienced individual (Goran, 2001; Short, 2002). The relationship is interactive and interpersonal and highlights the benefits of focused support in the workplace that enables individuals to realize their potential. In many professional groups the title mentor implies seniority, with responsibility for supporting new colleagues while they become established (Jarvis and Gibson, 1997). This responsibility may include a teaching role, but is more generally one of facilitation and access. The emphasis of the Macmillan Mentorship Training Programme (MMTP) is facilitation of role transition and career development. Morton-Cooper and Palmer's (2000) definition of a mentor therefore seems fitting:

> *'Someone who provides an enabling relationship that facilitates another's personal growth and development. The relationship is dynamic, reciprocal and can be emotionally intense. Within such a relationship the mentor assists with career development and guides the mentee through the organisational, social and political networks.'*

Contemporary mentorship

Interest in mentorship has been rejuvenated over the past 25–30 years. Initially interest developed within the realms of business, but more recently it has extended into education and healthcare arenas and feminist business organizations. Mentorship programmes have become more formalized in many disciplines, raising the profile and encouraging the adoption of mentorship programmes (Clutterbuck, 2001). Comprehensive national and international mentoring networks are developing at the same pace as technological advances, and online professional mentoring organizations appear to be economically viable ventures. Recently, there has been an extension of mentoring schemes into the spectrum of community projects to enhance opportunities for, and development of, disadvantaged groups of society (Clutterbuck, 2001).

There are various descriptions of mentorship and components of the role, including teacher, coach, role model, sponsor, adviser and guide (Goran, 2001). Whatever the professional, personal or educational focus, there is a shared conclusion that mentorship provides many benefits for mentor, mentee and the organization, as illustrated in *Table 3.1*.

Table 3.1: Benefits of mentorship

For the mentee	For the mentor	For the organization
Work-focused support		Increased staff security and morale. More staff with a sense of belonging to the organization
Facilitation of role transition	Opportunity to review own practice	Integrated staff members
Role security		
Personal and professional growth and development	Professional and personal development	
	Pride in watching others develop	
Political and strategic power development	Sharing of experience and knowledge	Professional staff with ability to utilize power and strategic awareness appropriately
		Sharing of organizational culture, values and commitment
Empowerment	Positively challenged and stimulated, encouraging reflective practice	Empowered, motivated, autonomous skilled workforce
	Development of new ideas	
Increased motivation	Increased stimulation and motivation	Motivated workforce
Increased job satisfaction and commitment to stay	Increased job satisfaction	Satisfied workforce Retention of staff
Improved knowledge base, with bridging of the practice–theory gap and development of critical thinking skills	Reciprocal learning, keeping practice up to date	
Enhanced competence		
Greater productivity		Improved staff efficacy
Career development		
Increased self-esteem	Increased self-esteem	More confident workforce
Enhanced socialization into new organization and organizational insight		Earlier socialization of individuals able to contribute to the organization and subscribe to, and promote, the organization's goals

Sources: Alvarado *et al*, 2003; Bhagia and Tinsley, 2000; Brown, 1999; Busen and Engebretson, 1999; Field, 2004; Goran, 2001; Prevosto, 2001; Ronsten *et al*, 2005; Rosser and King, 2003; Rosser *et al*, 2004; Sachdeva, 1996; Smith *et al*, 2001

The role of mentorship in developing healthcare professionals

Healthcare professionals have always emphasized the practical aspect of their work, and the value of practice-based learning has been maintained through multiple changes in education although the importance attached to it may have waned at times. Educationalists have become increasingly concerned with identifying effective ways of supporting healthcare students in their clinical placements, as current educational philosophies seek to reduce the theory–practice gap. Facilitation of learning in practice areas through mentorship may enable this (Cahill, 1996; Jarvis and Gibson, 1997; United Kingdom Central Council for Nursing, Midwifery and Health Visiting [UKCC], 1999).

One major benefit of working with a practice-based mentor is that the mentor is at the practice–theory interface. For this reason, and many others, there has been renewed interest in mentorship within the healthcare professions, revisiting the long-acknowledged benefits of mentorship and espousing the value of mentorship to professional development. Field (2004) states that excellent mentor support is vital to enabling nurses to progress. The majority of the current literature discusses the development of mentorship in the nursing profession, although there is some acknowledgement of the benefits across health care (Butterworth, 1997). There is increasing evidence of the development of mentorship schemes in medicine (Ansbacher, 2003; Katz *et al*, 1997; Sachdeva, 1996) and the physical therapy disciplines (Paschal *et al*, 2002; MacDonald *et al*, 2002) and there is even evidence of multidisciplinary mentorship within health care (Wrightson, 2001).

In the field of nursing, the increasing emphasis on developing competency of student nurses in order to achieve fitness for practice (UKCC, 1999) demands that the role of mentor for pre-registration nurses has a heavy assessment responsibility. The Nursing and Midwifery Council (NMC) (2002) stipulates that mentors for pre-registration nurses should be experienced and knowledgeable nurses, committed to creating a learning environment that will facilitate learning through effective role modelling, communication and working relationships in order to improve practice, and should be able to assess student performance. Interest in workplace support has recently been extended to incorporate support for registered nurses following the observations of the Department of Health (DH) (1999) and the UKCC (1999) that effective mentorship contributes to nurses' professional development.

The mentoring relationship

Beyond the academic confines of the previous descriptions, mentorship promotes a more global and long-term responsibility for the development of a mentee (Sachdeva,1996). For many the mentoring relationship comprises more personal, closer relationships, which demand time commitment and a level of emotional engagement (Bhagia and Tinsley, 2000). There is a consensus that the relationship between mentor and mentee is vital to a positive development experience; within that relationship a number of desirable qualities of a mentor have been identified, as listed in *Table 3.2.*

Table 3.2: Desirable qualities of a mentor

- Enthusiastic and motivated
- Genuine interest/belief in mentee and willing to commit to the relationship
- Approachable and generous with his/her time
- Willing to listen
- Able to challenge constructively and to provide constructive feedback
- Knowledgeable and able to facilitate reflective discussions
- Supportive, patient, understanding and affirming
- Visionary
- Consistent
- Respectful
- Friendly and welcoming
- Willing to share and to collaborate
- Strong leadership, communication and interpersonal skills

Sources: Alvarado *et al,* 2003; Busen and Engebretson, 1999; Cahill, 1996; Darling, 1984; Earnshaw, 1995; Goran, 2001; Gray and Smith, 2000; Phillips *et al,* 1996a,b; Spouse, 1996

Mentors may present challenges to some mentees in the workplace, serving as gatekeepers to clinical experience (Spouse, 1996) or creating a sense of disempowering conformity or oppressive protectiveness (Cahill, 1996; Earnshaw, 1995; Gray and Smith, 2000). Arbitrary pairing of mentors and mentees can produce personality clashes or allocation to unwilling mentors (Andrews and Chilton, 2000; Earnshaw, 1995; Phillips *et al*, 1996a,b). It is important that mentors are willing to be involved in support and are given adequate preparation for their role. To optimize the mentoring relationship, mentors need formal preparation and continued support for a complex and demanding role; its absence is a recurring theme in the literature (Andrews and Chilton, 2000; Duffy *et al*, 2000; Phillips *et al*, 1996a,b). However, the NMC (2002) clearly states that mentors 'will require preparation for, and support in, their role'. Mentors who have experienced formal preparation for their role rate themselves more highly as mentors than mentors who have had no preparation (Andrews and Chilton, 2000; Duffy *et al*, 2000).

There is increasing evidence that mentorship eases the transition of qualified nurses to new posts and advanced roles. Although mentorship for students and newly qualified nurses is relatively well established, formal support for those making the transition to specialist practice is sporadic and often informal and unstructured (Bamford and Gibson, 2000). While there is retention of an element of supporting formal work-based learning, the emphasis in mentoring post-registration nurses, and nurse teachers, is one of facilitating transition, enhancing socialization and familiarity, and optimizing performance within a new environment through experiential learning (Alvarado *et al*, 2003; Bower, 2000; Brown, 1999; Ronsten *et al*, 2005; Rosser and King, 2003; Short, 2002). This is the direction encouraged in the MMTP; the aim is to formalize the support provided for new specialists within a structured framework of learning and development for both mentor and mentee. Macmillan mentors are, as Daloz (1999) suggests, encouraged to:

'... hang around through transitions, a foot on either side of the gulf; they offer a hand to help us swing across'.

The MMTP encourages mentors to be present alongside new specialist practitioners, providing vital support in a new role while challenging their practice constructively to encourage the development of new skills.

In order to maximize professional growth, there needs to be a balance between levels of support and challenge, or stretching and nurturing; overuse of either inhibits optimal growth (Clutterbuck, 2001; Daloz, 1999). If the mentor takes control of the relationship, it dissolves into a didactic, disempowering relationship for the mentee. If, on the other hand, mentees are encouraged to take the initiative in the relationship, the relationship is relatively 'non-directional' and the mentee develops self-reliance as one of the many skills in his/her development, encouraging a proactive approach to learning and development (Clutterbuck, 2001).

Models of mentorship

Mentorship embraces a variety of models, including traditional apprenticeship schemes, training models to ensure development of skills and competence, and collaborative reflective practice models that focus on developing the whole person. There is a variety of approaches to establishing the mentoring relationship, ranging from the classic, self-selecting relationships of attraction, which persist for years, to the more formal, constructed and facilitated mentorship contracts (Morton-Cooper and Palmer, 2000; Murray, 1991).

Darling (1984) speaks of a classic mentoring relationship founded on initial attraction, admiration for that person or a wish to emulate aspects of his/her character or performance. The mentee approaches the person and inquires whether or not that person might be willing to mentor him/her. If the person is willing to act as mentor, it is vital that he/she invests time and energy in supporting the mentee and demonstrates positive regard and respect for the mentee if the relationship is going to yield positive results. The relationship is one of inspiration, investment and support. Contracted mentoring relationships occur when a mentee is assigned a designated mentor for a specified period; a successful contractual mentoring relationship may extend into a lasting, classic relationship.

In healthcare education and professional development, there is often the need for a facilitated/contractual mentorship relationship of limited duration. The MMTP was devised from this philosophical angle: to facilitate the transition of generalist practitioners to the specialist role through provision of a 12-month, formal programme of instruction, clarification and support. The MMTP offers mentorship from practitioners with limited power advantages but greater knowledge and experience of the specialist role with which to guide the new practitioner (Goran, 2001). The focus of the MMTP is not the teaching or assessment of skills leading to clinical competence, but support of newcomers to develop the non-clinical aspects of the specialist role and to gain organizational, political and professional knowledge, with a view to facilitating socialization, thus easing the role transition. Experiential learning, through which mentees are encouraged to reflect upon their practice, is central to role development. This reflective practice enables new specialists to develop skills, knowledge and awareness that enhance role transition and prompt specialist functioning of greater maturity and expertise (Jarvis and Gibson, 1997).

Acknowledging the benefits of reflective practice and appropriate challenging, members of MNIE felt that Morton-Cooper and Palmer's (2000) 'reflective practitioner model and mentor as critical friend' was the most appropriate mentorship model to facilitate transition and development into specialist roles.

This model encourages the establishment of a trusting relationship in which mentor and mentee work closely together, facilitating reflective practice with appropriate challenging and collaborative inquiry into work-based situations. Both mentor and mentee benefit, developing their own knowledge, skills and wisdom (Clutterbuck, 2001). This relationship is perhaps more suggestive of the mentoring relationships utilized in business and commerce rather than the traditional educational mentoring roles most dominant in nursing.

The Macmillan Mentorship Training Programme

Rationale

MNIE believes very strongly that being an effective mentor is a vital function of experienced specialist practitioners, and that an effective mentor can significantly help the newly appointed specialist practitioner to make a successful transition to the specialist role. While clinical supervision is indicative of good practice, mentorship is an additional formalized supportive relationship, which focuses on personal and professional growth and development.

The MMTP was developed to address the needs of both new specialist practitioners and experienced clinical nurse specialists (CNSs). It aimed to address some of the issues related to role transition discussed in the previous chapter, eg. time management, working autonomously with a clinical caseload and responding to the expectations of others. The other aim was to prepare experienced CNSs for the role of mentor, providing formal support and learning opportunities for them throughout the mentoring relationship.

Early development of the MMTP was initiated by a group of Macmillan service development managers and clinical specialists in the North of England who were forming a group to see what could be done to support those new to the specialist role, and those expected to be providing mentorship support to new specialists. Lecturers from MNIE were invited to join the group and it was agreed that utilizing the existing expertise within the clinical community would be a good way forward. This would not only provide support to new specialists from experienced practitioners, but would also provide an opportunity for experienced practitioners to develop new skills. The mentorship relationship is a partnership that can lead to the personal and professional development of both individuals (Morton-Cooper and Palmer, 2000), and so the MMTP was born.

It was agreed to develop and pilot a training programme, utilizing a formalized mentorship system that would prepare experienced Macmillan CNSs willing to undertake the role. Support roles need to be introduced effectively and applied appropriately, whatever the nature of the role or context (Morton-Cooper and Palmer, 2000), so it was anticipated that new postholders would be offered a mentor when they came into post. Unless the new postholder was able to identify his/her own mentor who met the criteria, the Macmillan service development manager and the Macmillan lecturer identified a potentially suitable mentor, initiating the formal contract mentorship previously discussed. The criteria for those willing to act as mentor were:

- a minimum of 1 year's experience in their current role
- willingness to participate in the MMTP
- able to provide evidence of continuous professional development
- support from their line manager
- a minimum of 2 years' experience as a specialist practitioner.

The 'contract' was to last 12 months, but could be extended if both parties were in agreement. For the purposes of the pilot the evaluation was undertaken at 12 months. Results of the evaluation of the pilot programme will be presented later in the chapter.

Structure of the MMTP

The MMTP has three key components:

- a 2-day training workshop
- six to eight weekly action learning groups
- an active mentorship relationship with a designated mentee.

The MMTP is underpinned by the following core themes: effective mentorship, experiential learning/action learning, and reflective practice.

Two-day workshop

The workshop utilizes a range of teaching methods, including small group work and reflection, to explore models of role transition, the principles of mentorship, the key attributes of the mentor, models of reflective practice and experiential learning. Participants are encouraged to discuss these topics in the light of their own experiences when they were new to the specialist role. They are also encouraged to view the relationship as one of mutual learning rather than assuming that they, the experienced practitioner, would purely be giving advice. Mentees are invited to the first day of the workshop, where role transition, reflective practice and the mentorship model underpinning the programme are explored together to ensure common understanding.

The MMTP mentorship relationship

This is a key element in the learning process for the mentor, during which he/she develops and utilizes the knowledge and skills explored through the 2-day workshop. Much of the learning is experiential, occurring throughout the course of the relationship. For this reason the concept of action learning groups was introduced and will be discussed later in the chapter. Action learning has some similarities to the experiential learning cycle identified by Kolb (1984) (Lee, 1999). Some of the mentors and mentees may not have met before and the 2-day workshop offers an opportunity to meet and begin to get to know each other, and on a more practical level arrange mentorship meetings. We usually advise mentors and mentees to set up several meetings in advance, otherwise it will become increasingly difficult to fit them in.

Three key stages are identified in the mentorship relationship (Morton-Cooper and Palmer, 2000): the initiation, development and termination phases. Each phase requires investment, of different types, as the mentee moves from a level of dependency to a level of independence.

- Initiation phase: This is the 'getting to know you' phase, i.e. beginning to establish the relationship. An important task at the outset is setting the ground rules, clarifying boundaries and issues of confidentiality. The length of this phase will vary with the individuals but may take up to 3 months. It is important that the mentor and mentee have regular contact during this time.

- Development phase: This is the working phase of the relationship, during which there is increasing trust and the focus is on individual growth and development. It is during this phase that new CNSs will begin to develop confidence in their knowledge and skills and over time should become increasingly independent, developing the confidence to be creative and to experiment with risk taking.

■ Termination phase: Towards the end of the relationship (12–18 months) the CNS should have further developed his/her knowledge and skills and be able to function with increased confidence, able to act independently on his/her own initiative. A good mentorship relationship has the potential to end as a positive professional friendship and in some instances may develop into a new phase of clinical supervision. If this should happen, then new boundaries and ground rules should be established.

Experiential and action learning

Following the 2-day workshop, action learning groups or sets facilitate the process of learning and support for mentors. The key characteristic of an action learning set is the focus on the individual and his/her future action. Action learning was first explored as a learning technique by Revans (1983) and has been described as simply learning by doing. Action learning is based on the relationship between action and reflection, and it has been suggested that this is an effective way of developing and utilizing reflection to develop clinical practice (Haddock, 1997). It is a social process whereby those involved learn with and from each other. McGill and Beaty(1995) define action learning as:

> '... a continuous process of learning and reflection supported by colleagues with the intention of getting things done.'

The main aim is to create an environment in which the individual is encouraged to seek solutions to problems utilizing a reflective process, supported by the group. A study by Kirrane (2001) concluded that the use of action learning encouraged the use of reflective processes, which may have an impact on clinical outcomes. Choice and the recognition of the need to learn/develop underpin participation. The action learning model has been utilized to develop leadership skills in healthcare professionals (Rayner *et al*, 2002; Taylor *et al*, 2000), to facilitate the student learning experience (Heidari and Galvin, 2003) and to break down the inter-agency and interprofessional barriers that can prevent effective practice (Randall *et al*, 2000).

An action learning set is more than a support group: although members are there to provide support for one another in finding a way forward with their issues or difficulties, they are also there to challenge and can take a more assertive role. The responsibility for resolving the issue remains firmly with the individual (McGill and Beaty, 1995). Action learning sets enable individuals to be challenged in an observable and safe environment, facilitating analyses of personal perceptions of the issues and the views of other group members. This in turn can enable individuals to approach problems with the confidence to make the necessary changes (Rayner *et al*, 2002).

Structure of action learning sets

Action learning has four elements:

- The person: Each individual needs to commit to taking part fully in the group. Once committed to the concept, this needs to be borne out in practice with priority and commitment given to attending and participating in the group.

- The project: The projects that individuals work on should be what Revans (1983) interprets as problems. Problems are those issues, challenges and opportunities where there is no single answer, no single way of doing things. Each individual contributes by bringing the problem or issue that he/she wants to take some further action on. Examples that came up regularly were: facilitating awareness of the wider aspects of the specialist role; the tendency to over-supervise; coping with having his/her own practice challenged; and moving the mentee to a place of independence.

- The group: Meeting together to think through difficult issues and identifying ways forward. Group members learn from each other as these issues and problems are explored and further actions are agreed within the context of challenge and support.

- The coming together of the action and the learning: Having analysed issues and thought through the way forward with the help of others in the group, the individual then acts to resolve his/her problems. Each mentor would take away some specific action points to facilitate resolution of the issue during the next meeting with his/her mentee, and be prepared to give feedback at the next meeting.

Preparation for the meeting may include the following questions (McGill and Beaty, 1995):

- My previous action points were...?
- What have I done since the last meeting?

- What do I want to spend time on at this set meeting?
- How much time do I think I need?

Allocation of time within the action learning set is important. The group might begin with half an hour of general discussion and 'catching up'. As recommended, each group member is allocated half an hour to present and invite discussion from other members of the group (McGill and Beaty, 1995). Individuals who think they may need more time need to negotiate this with the other group members. Breaks are incorporated into the time to provide the group with an opportunity to re-energize.

The mentors agree their own action learning meeting dates, which are arranged for the whole year. Members undertake a commitment to attend all of the meetings. It is important that the group establishes clear ground rules at the outset, concerning, for example, confidentiality, respect, openness, and mobile phones being switched off. The size of the groups varies, but there are usually about eight members. Six to eight is the recommended number for small group working (McGill and Beaty, 1995; Weinstein, 1995). Meetings last approximately 4 hours with breaks; however, for those who have to travel a significant distance, this could mean the whole day, which is a significant time commitment.

The groups are facilitated by one of the Macmillan lecturers, although the group could, in addition, nominate a chairperson if it wished. The facilitator can play a key role in encouraging each individual to take responsibility for presenting his/her issues and taking away an action plan (McGill and Beaty, 1995). The facilitator can also help to create a safe environment where set members feel able to bring sensitive issues or problems (Haddock, 1997). Initially the groups tend to be quite dependent on the facilitator and in the initial phases the skill of the facilitator is key (Rayner *et al*, 2002); however, as group members grow in confidence and experience, the facilitator plays less of a role and in some instances the group may become self-facilitating. The action learning sets during the MMTP are facilitated throughout. This approach ensures that the group stays on track. The evaluation indicated that the mentors felt that learning was enhanced when a facilitator was present.

The action learning sets have proved very popular with the mentors, who showed a high degree of commitment to attending, despite the time constraints and travelling involved. Many of them have utilized the action learning format to take forward projects in their own workplace. The MMTP programme is now delivered in Macmillan education units across the UK, and the results of a formal evaluation of the first programmes, delivered in three units, are presented and discussed below.

Evaluation of the MMTP

Effective evaluation of programmes can inform decision-making and influence the development of new educational initiatives (Chambers, 1988; Ferguson, 1994; Parfitt, 1986). Although definitions of evaluation vary across the literature, there is a consensus that the purpose of evaluation is mainly concerned with establishing the worth, value or merit of something (Clarke and Dawson, 1999; Scriven, 1996) by applying a formal, systematic approach to the collection, analysis and dissemination of data (Clarke and Dawson, 1999). The focus of the MMTP evaluation was to assess the extent to which the programme was operating as intended (process or implementation evaluation) and the extent to which the programme was achieving its outcomes (outcome evaluation) (Patton, 1996).

Design and method

The evaluation adopted a non-experimental formative approach, which utilized self-report postal questionnaires comprising a range of measures. Open and closed questions and rating and Likert-type scales were developed, allowing qualitative and quantitative data to be collected. The advantages and disadvantages of the use of questionnaires have been widely reported (Malby, 1995; Robson, 2002); however, it was decided that this was the most expedient method to use, taking into account the geographical location of the subjects.

Different questionnaires were developed for each subject group to determine whether the programme outcomes had been achieved and to evaluate the operational processes of the MMTP from the different vantage points of key stakeholders in the project. Validity of the questionnaire was established by submission to a panel of experts. Reliability was not tested. The questionnaires were distributed to all stakeholders shortly after the mentors had completed their 12-month programme of action learning.

Sample

The sample consisted of 26 mentor/mentee pairs (26 mentors and 26 mentees who had participated in the MMTP at three Macmillan education units), the mentors' managers (26) and Macmillan service development managers (SDMs) (26).

Analysis and discussion of results

A total of 88% (23) of mentees, 96% (25) of mentors, 54% (14) of managers and 27% (7) of Macmillan SDMs returned completed questionnaires. Excel analysis of the quantitative data generated descriptive (frequency and percentage) statistics. Qualitative data were collected from each of the open-ended questionnaires, and thematic analysis identified five themes:

- personal development
- developing others
- mentorship role
- relationships
- benefits.

Achievement of programme outcomes

Being prepared for the role

Almost all mentors (91%) felt well prepared for the mentorship role, identifying increased confidence in knowledge and skills (96%), including ability to give feedback (83%), establishing mentorship relationships, working within contract boundaries and understanding of role transition. This was endorsed by the mentees, 72% of whom felt that their mentor was well prepared for the role.

All of the mentees (100%) agreed that support from a mentor was important during transition. Benefits to the mentee were established from a variety of sources and highlighted the importance of the relationship:

> *"Time spent addressing my issues regarding my role helped me identify improvements/increased confidence in myself and role. This may not have happened so quickly if my mentor had not been available." (mentee)*

This was endorsed by a line manager, who also clearly demonstrated not only the personal benefits for the mentee but also benefit to the service and ultimately the user (patient):

> *"The mentee has been pivotal in developing a new service with a strong influence of evidence-based practice ... I believe that the mentorship relationship has given her the confidence to deal with day-to-day issues." (line manager)*

It could be argued that confidence can only develop within a relationship based on trust – a tenet of the Morton-Cooper and Palmer (2000) model of mentorship, where success, mistakes and failure can be explored safely. This is facilitated by use of the model and also by the inclusion of role transition within the programme. Both might contribute towards closure of the perception gap between mentor and mentee. For example, mentors consciously revisiting their own transition experiences within a theoretical framework may develop an understanding of the mentee's position (O'Connor, 2001). Theoretically, therefore, and hopefully in reality the perceptual gap diminishes, resulting in mutual understanding, communication and support between mentors and mentees. It could be suggested that this increased appreciation of each other's needs is akin to some definitions of empathy explored in Kunyk (2001). This new appreciation may explain some of the perceived benefits of mentorship identified by the mentees, and the value of exploring both the models of transition (74%) and mentorship (81%) for the mentor.

Identifying their own learning and development needs

Of the 26 mentors, 78% were able to identify their own learning and development needs following the mentorship programme:

> *"The programme addressed my development needs as a mentor. I have been mentoring CNSs for a long time without understanding the process."*

This was endorsed by managers, whose perceptions of the benefits of the programme included an increase in mentors' awareness of the wider components of the specialist role, sharing of best practice and dissemination of skills The mentors not only identified areas for personal development but also acknowledged the affirming nature of the programme:

> *"It made me realize that I had skills to pass onto people."*

> *"... provided affirmation and increased confidence in abilities."*

In an educational era of distance, self-directed e-learning and web-based learning, the advantages of networking and mutual learning may not be seen as cost-effective or even best educational practice. However, 74% of mentors found the action learning sets valuable and supported their continued inclusion in the programme despite the practical difficulties of attending:

"I gained further experience in problem solving and benefited from new ways of learning, eg. action learning groups, where I was able to contribute to and access the knowledge and experience of other experienced CNSs."

All mentors (100%) found sharing experiences with other mentors to be valuable. This is supported by Kuiper and Persut (2004), who cite Davies' (1995) view that sharing experiences with peers and teachers in a non-judgmental milieu is essential for effective reflection, as barriers may develop with experience, eg. denial of not knowing and satisfaction with own level of performance (Hancock, 1998; Heath, 1998). Whether support has to be provided face to face will be a challenge for the ongoing development of the MMTP, with enhanced rigour of evaluation of MNIE programmes and emerging evidence of the benefits of other forms of learning (Atack, 2003; Kenny, 2002).

Conclusion

Mentorship has been demonstrated to benefit transition experiences, and the MMTP does prepare mentors to support new postholders in the transition to specialist practitioner. New skills are acquired and affirmation of existing qualities is received by mentor and mentee. These have benefited not only the individual, the team and the service but also, indirectly, the patient. This has been achieved by the balance between a theoretical framework and learning strategies that utilize and build upon an individual's existing experience, knowledge and skills. Qualitative evaluation of the action learning sets may deepen understanding of the mentors' experiential learning.

It will be interesting to see what impact e-learning has on the MMTP, which currently relies heavily on face-to-face contact. Will a web-based course and the use of chat rooms remove the need for personal meetings? With the demise of the national boards, might the MMTP be adapted by the partnership HEIs to provide an acceptable replacement for the old national boards teaching and assessing courses? This could incorporate aspects of assessment that currently lie outside the responsibilities of the Macmillan mentors.

References

Alvarado K, Keatings M, Dorsay JP (2003) Cultivating APNs for the future: a hospital-based advanced practice nursing internship program. *Can J Nurs Leadersh* **16**(1): 91–8

Andrews M, Chilton F (2000) Student and mentor perceptions of mentoring effectiveness. *Nurse Educ Today* **20**(7): 555–62

Ansbacher R (2003) A guest editorial: the mentor-mentee relationship. *Obstet Gynec Surv* **58**(8): 505–6

Atack L (2003) Becoming a web-based learner: registered nurses' experience. *Journal of Advanced Learning* **44**(3): 289–97

Bamford O, Gibson F (2000) The clinical nurse specialist: perceptions of practising CNSs of their role and development needs. *J Clin Nurs* **9**(2): 282–92

Bhagia J, Tinsley JA (2000) The mentoring partnership. *Mayo Clin Proc* **75**(5): 535–7

Bower FL (2000) Succession planning: a strategy for taking charge. *Nurs Leadersh Forum* **4**(4): 110–14

Brown HN (1999) Mentoring new faculty. *Nurse Educ* **24**(1): 48–51

Busen NH, Engebretson J (1999) Mentoring in advanced practice nursing: the use of metaphor in concept exploration. *Internet Journal of Advanced Nursing Practice* **2**(2): 10

Butterworth T (1997) *It is Good to Talk: An evaluation of clinical supervision and mentorship in England and Scotland.* University of Manchester

Cahill HA (1996) A qualitative analysis of student nurses' experiences of mentorship. *J Adv Nurs* **24**(4): 791–9

Chambers M (1988) Curriculum evaluation: an approach towards appraising a post-basic psychiatric course. *J Adv Nurs* **13**(3): 330–40

Clarke A, Dawson R (1999) *Evaluation Research: An introduction to principles, methods and practice.* Sage, London

Clutterbuck D (2001) *Everyone Needs a Mentor: Fostering talent at work.* 3rd edn. Chartered Institute of Personnel and Development, London

Darling LW (1984) What do nurses want in a mentor? *J Nurs Admin* **14**(10): 42–4

Davies E (1995) Reflective practice: a focus for caring. *J Nurs Educ* **34**(4): 167–74

Daloz LA (1999) *Mentor: Guiding the journey of adult learners.* Jossey-Bass, San Francisco

Department of Health (1999) *Making a Difference: Strengthening the nursing, midwifery and health visiting contribution to health and healthcare.* DH, London

Duffy K, Docherty C, Cardnuff L *et al* (2000) The nurse lecturer's role in mentoring the mentors. *Nurs Stand* **15**(6): 35–8

Earnshaw G (1995) Mentorship: the students' views. *Nurse Educ Today* **15**(4): 274–9

Field DE (2004) Moving from novice to expert – the value of learning in clinical practice: a literature review. *Nurse Educ Today* **24**(7): 560–5

Ferguson A (1994) Evaluating the purpose and benefits of continuing education in nursing and the implications for the provision of continuing education for cancer nurses. *J Adv Nurs* **19**(4): 640–6

Goran SF (2001) Mentorship as a teaching strategy. *Crit Care Nurs Clin North Am* **13**(1): 119–29

Gray MA, Smith LN (2000) The qualities of an effective mentor from the student nurse's perspective: findings from a longitudinal qualitative study. *J Adv Nurs* **32**(6): 1542–9

Haddock J (1997) Reflection in groups: contextual and theoretical considerations within nurse education and practice. *Nurse Educ Today* **17**(5): 381–5

Hancock P (1998) Reflective practice – using a learning journal. *Nurs Stand* **13**(17): 37–40

Heath H (1998) Reflection and patterns of knowing in nursing. *J Adv Nurs* **27**(5): 1054–9

Heidari F, Galvin K (2003) Action learning groups: can they help students develop their knowledge and skills? *Nurse Education in Practice* **3**: 49–55

Jarvis P, Gibson S (1997) *The Teacher Practitioner and Mentor in Nursing, Midwifery, Health Visiting and the Social Services.* 2nd edn. Stanley Thornes, Cheltenham

Katz AM, Siegel BS, Rappo P (1997) Reflections from a collaborative pediatric mentorship programme: building a community of resources. *Ambulatory Child Health* **3**: 101–12

Kenny A (2002) Online learning: enhancing nurse education? *J Adv Nurs* **38**(2): 127–35

Kirrane C (2001) Using action learning in reflective practice. *Prof Nurse* **16**(5): 1102–5

Kolb DA (1984) *Experiential Learning: Experience as the source of learning and development.* Prentice Hall, Englewood Cliffs, NJ

Kuiper R, Persut D (2004) Promoting cognitive and metacognitive reflective reasoning skills in nursing practice: self-regulated learning theory. *J Adv Nurs* **45**(4): 381–91

Kunyk J (2001) Clarification of conceptualizations of empathy. *J Adv Nurs* **35**(3): 317–25

Lee NJ (1999) A beginner's guide to action learning. *Nurs Times* **3**(6): 52–3

MacDonald CA, Cox PD, Bartlett DJ *et al* (2002) Consensus on methods to foster physical therapy professional behaviours. *Journal of Physical Therapy Education* **16**(1): 27–36

Malby R (Ed) (1995) *Clinical Audit for Nurses and Therapists.* Scutari Press, London

McGill I, Beaty L (1995) *Action Learning: A guide for professional, management and educational development.* 2nd edn. Kogan Page, London

Morton-Cooper A, Palmer A (2000) *Mentorship, Preceptorship and Clinical Supervision: A guide to professional support roles in clinical practice.* 2nd edn. Blackwell Science, Oxford

Murray M (1991) *Beyond the Myths and Magic of Mentoring.* Jossey-Bass, San Francisco, California

NMC (2002) *Standards for the Preparation of Teachers of Nursing and Midwifery.* NMC, London

O'Connor J (2001) *The NLP Workbook.* Harper Collins, London

Parfitt B (1986) Steps in evaluating a programme of nurse education. *Nurse Educ Today* **6**(4): 166–71

Paschal KA, Jensen GM, Mostrom E (2002) Building portfolios: a means for developing habits of reflective practice in physical therapy education. *Journal of Physical Therapy Education* **16**(3): 38–53

Patton MQ (1996) A world larger than formative and summative. *Eval Pract* **17**(2): 131–44

Phillips RM, Davies WB, Neary M (1996a) The practitioner-teacher: a study in the introduction of mentors in the preregistration education programme in Wales: Part 1. *J Adv Nurs* **23**(5): 1037–44

Phillips RM, Davies WB, Neary M (1996b) The practitioner-teacher: a study in the introduction of mentors in the pre-registration education programme in Wales: Part 2. *J Adv Nurs* **23**(6): 1080–8

Prevosto P (2001) The effect of 'mentored' relationships on satisfaction and intent to stay of company-grade US Army Reserve nurses. *Mil Med* **166**(1): 21–6

Randall J, Cowley P, Tomlinson P (2000) Overcoming barriers to effective practice in child care. *Child and Family Social Work* **5**: 343–52

Rayner D, Chisholm H, Appleby H (2002) Developing leadership through action learning. *Nurs Stand* **16**(29): 37–9

Revans R (1983) *The Origins and Growth of Action Learning.* Chartwell Brant, Bromley

Roberts A (1999) *Homer's Mentor – Duties fulfilled or misconstrued.* Available at http://home.att.net/~nickols/homers_mentor.htm (accessed 21.03.06)

Robson C (2002) *Real World Research.* Blackwell Publishing, Oxford

Ronsten B, Anderson E, Gustafsson B (2005) Confirming mentorship. *J Nurs Manag* **13**(4): 312–21

Rosser M, King L (2003) Transition experiences of qualified nurses moving into hospice nursing. *J Adv Nurs* **43**(2): 206–15

Rosser M, Rice AM, Campbell H, Jack C (2004) Evaluation of a mentorship programme for specialist practitioners. *Nurse Educ Today* **24**(8): 596–604

Sachdeva AK (1996) Preceptorship, mentorship and the adult learner in medical and health sciences education. *J Cancer Educ* **11**(3): 131–6

Scriven M (1996) The theory behind practical evaluation. *Evaluation* **2**(4): 393–404

Short JD (2002) Mentoring: career enhancement for occupational and environmental health nurses. *AAOHN J* **50**(3): 135–43

Smith LS, McAllister LE, Snype Crawford C (2001) Mentoring benefits and issues for public health nurses. *Public Health Nurs* **18**(2): 101–7

Spouse J (1996) The effective mentor: a model for student-centred learning in clinical practice. *Nursing Times Research* **1**(2):120–33

Taylor R, Illing J, Stewart J, O'Halloran C (2000) The development of clinical governance leads. An educational initiative – applying theory to practice. *Journal of Clinical Governance* **8**: 202–6

UKCC (1999) *Fitness for Practice.* The UKCC Commission for Nursing and Midwifery Education (chaired by Sir Leonard Peach). UKCC, London

Weinstein K (1995) *Action Learning: A journey in discovery and development.* Harper Collins, London

Wrightson J (2001) Multidisciplinary mentorship in practice. *Pract Midwife* **4**(9): 19–21

CHAPTER 4

Preparing for role transition – how does one become a specialist?

Ann Marie Rice, Brian Nyatanga, Heather Campbell, Megan Rosser

This chapter explores the concept of role transition and makes some suggestions about support structures that may support and facilitate transition. Role transition occurs any time an individual experiences any change in his/her employment status, and does not necessarily mean a new job (Glen and Waddington, 1998; Nicholson, 1984). While responding to the many changes in the healthcare environment, individuals may undergo a number of changes in the expectations of their role; indeed, the role itself may not change outwardly and may have no change in title. In many ways this can be the most difficult type of transition as it remains hidden and is often unacknowledged by the organization, making it difficult for the individual to seek appropriate support. However, it may be useful to look first at the development of specialist practice from a historical perspective.

Historical perspective

The concept of the nurse as a clinical specialist is not new and was first described by Francis Reiter in 1943 (Reiter, 1966). The role of clinical nurse specialist (CNS) first appeared in the USA in the 1950s, and by the 1960s could also be found in Canada (Bousfield, 1997). The value of the CNS role was perceived to be the linking of theory to clinical practice. In order to facilitate this, the first degree programmes in nursing were developed; these enabled nurses to practise at this advanced level by embedding scientific theory into clinical practice. The first programme for CNSs was developed in the USA by Hildegard Peplau in 1952 (Montemuro, 1987).

The concept of a CNS was not developed in the UK until the 1980s (Castledine, 1982). In the 1960s, changes in the traditional role of the nurse were typified by a few administrative posts, and it was not until the implementation of the Salmon Report in 1966 that the managerial role was combined with clinical expertise in the emergence of the nursing officer (Bousfield, 1997). Reorganizations of the NHS in 1974 placed increasing emphasis on administration and management as the key functions of the nursing officer. This development raised concern that nurses were not being allowed to develop clinical skills and expertise at a more senior level, and that this would have implications for the standards of care (Royal College of Nursing [RCN], 1974). The RCN held a seminar in 1975 at which the need for a CNS role was identified; the role was deemed necessary in order to provide a clinical career structure for nurses in clinical practice that would maintain and improve standards of clinical care (RCN, 1981a,b). Despite the increasing numbers of specialist posts developed in the 1980s, there was little direction or understanding of what the criteria for these posts should be (Castledine 1982, 2004).

By the 1990s, many more CNS posts had been created. They have extended into a wide variety of specialties, including oncology, palliative care, diabetes, stroke and many others (Castledine, 2004; Jack *et al*, 2003; McGee *et al*, 1996). The study by McGee *et al* (1996) found that the most common domains of practice for CNSs were in the acute physical dimensions of care. Many of these posts were developed initially in response to publication of *The Scope of Professional Practice* (United Kingdom Central Council for Nursing, Midwifery and Health Visiting [UKCC], 1992), but increasingly are now being developed in response to the shortage of medical staff and the reduction in junior doctors' hours.

As the numbers of CNSs continue to increase, many of the new roles have developed in a more site-specific way. In some cases CNSs have taken on additional tasks that would previously have been undertaken by medical staff, such as administering minor treatments and carrying out diagnostic tests such as endoscopies and medical assessments (Castledine, 2004), with an increase in the number of nurse-led clinics to follow up and review patients. However, with the current climate around medical shortages and junior doctors' hours, there is a risk that the specialist nurse may develop along a medical model and it has been suggested that this is a result of the lack of national direction and a failure to define specialist practice (Castledine, 2004).

Defining specialist practice

A clear definition of specialist practice has been hindered by the plethora of titles currently in use. Confusion continues to exist, with titles such as CNS, nurse practitioner, advanced nurse practitioner, higher level practitioner and nurse consultant being used in the care setting, often with little consensus on the meaning (Daly and Carnwell, 2003). There is also a lack of clarity in the roles and responsibilities attached to these titles, with grades ranging from F to G and in some instances as high as I grade. This process of grading is now being superseded by *Agenda for Change* (Department of Health [DH], 2003a), but it is not yet known whether this will lead to greater clarity about the meaning of the term specialist practitioner. It is beyond the scope of this chapter to explore the various titles associated with advanced practice, and the focus here will be on specialist practice.

There is also evidence that the level of preparation varies enormously (Bousfield, 1997). This has implications for the ability of some individuals to fulfil the breadth of responsibilities of the role. As a result, there are many variations in the titles, range of skills, remit, level of responsibility, level of preparedness and subsequent place of the CNS within the organizational hierarchy. Role definitions have broadened and this has been exacerbated by the frequency with which individuals have been permitted to develop and operationalize the role, often with little direction from the organization; this has led to ambiguity for CNSs and the wider healthcare team (Loudermilk, 1990).

It has also been difficult at times to clarify the differences between the role of the generalist practitioner and that of the specialist practitioner, with many 'generalist' nurses working in specialist areas and, as a result, acquiring a certain level of specialist knowledge. However, some key differences have been identified between the two groups of nurses. Generalist nurses are more involved in the general care of the patient and are more likely to be working within a more structured ward or departmental routine. They generally work within agreed protocols and boundaries, and although they may be involved in developing and innovating practice, this is usually after consultation with the team. Generalist nurses are also likely to refer specialist healthcare problems (Castledine, 2003).

The clinical caseload has been identified as a key difference between generalist and specialist practitioners (Skilbeck *et al*, 2002). Specialist nurses are more likely to question the specialist aspects of the patient's care. They usually have a more flexible and autonomous working pattern, and some specialist services provide an on-call service and may have direct patient access. Specialist nurses are also prepared to challenge boundaries and will often act as a change agent, evaluating practice and trying out innovations. They are able to use their initiative, carry out advanced in-depth assessments of the patient's specialist needs and deal with specialist healthcare problems, working with generalists to solve them (Castledine, 2003). Specialist nurses also place an emphasis on the ability to work autonomously and see this as a key aspect of working as specialist practitioners (Glen and Waddington, 1998). However, as generalist nurses become more experienced and access education programmes, they are enabled to care for patients they would once have referred. As a result, the work of the specialist nurse becomes even more complex and challenging, demanding more sophisticated development opportunities.

The UKCC (1999a) defines the specialist practitioner as one who:

'... exercises higher levels of judgement and discretion in clinical care in order to function as a specialist.'

An earlier definition by Burwell (1989) states that:

'It [the specialist role] is a dynamic role for the nurse who has the ambition to transcend her traditional role of general patient care provider and become involved at a greater depth in a specialist area, applying highly refined skills and knowledge to evaluate and teach, serve as a role model, identify problems, research for answers and become involved in the decision-making process in the area of specific competence.'

So, how do we make sense of this situation and, more importantly, what do the general public understand about the level of expertise that is being provided when they are seen by a specialist practitioner? Work has been undertaken by the Nursing and Midwifery Council (NMC) (formerly the UKCC) to develop agreed competencies for specialist and advanced practice roles (Woods, 1998). This need for clarity and firm criteria was recognized by the UKCC (1999b) in *Fitness for Practice*. The NMC has recently completed a consultation on the role of the advanced practitioner – *Consultation on a Framework for the Standard of Post-Registration Nursing* (NMC, 2005) – and is expected to publish criteria later this year. It is anticipated that the title 'advanced practitioner' will appear on the register by 2010.

Jack *et al* (2003) suggest that there are between 60 and 320 areas of specialist practice and that this is associated with an attempt to establish a workable definition for the term CNS. With the emergence of these new roles, the UKCC published *The Scope of Professional Practice* in 1992. This document allowed nurses to define the limits of their practice, and provided that they acquired the relevant education and training and accepted individual responsibility they could become involved in almost any area of healthcare practice (Daly and Carnwell, 2003). However, inconsistencies in job descriptions and expectations of the role across different healthcare organizations make it difficult for nurses to do this (Castledine, 2004; Loudermilk, 1990). Despite local and post-specific differences, role titles, levels of role competencies and clinical autonomy should remain constant and discernible. In an attempt to achieve this, some authors have identified a number of components and competencies related to the specialist role.

Components of specialist practice

The hallmarks of specialist practice have been identified as higher levels of enquiry, advanced clinical decision-making and expertise in the provision of clinical care (Benner, 1984; Hamric and Spross, 1989; Redmond, 2000; UKCC, 1999). The specialist practitioner is expected to have not only expertise in the clinical area, but also skills in leadership, management, research and education (Tackenberg and Rausch, 1995). More recent literature identifies similar components, including expert practice, consultancy, education, research, administration and acting as a change agent (Bamford and Gibson, 2000; Redekopp, 1997).

Some authors have attempted to establish the differences and similarities between the CNS and nurse practitioner roles, identifying a series of core competencies common to both roles (Daly and Carnwell, 2003). They suggest that CNSs work closely with medical specialties and see patients in which an initial diagnosis or differentiation of condition has been made, whereas nurse practitioners practise independently and receive patients with undiagnosed health problems. This emphasizes the need for role clarity between the various nursing roles associated with advanced practice.

The American Nurses Association adopted a set of criteria for specialist practice, which was developed from the literature and summarized by Girard (1987) as:

- a practitioner who is involved in direct patient care
- a practitioner who is involved in the education of patients, relatives and staff
- a practitioner who can act as a consultant for other nurses and other disciplines/professions
- a practitioner who is a researcher within his/her own area of specialist practice

- a practitioner who is able to fulfil the role of change agent
- a practitioner who is able to assume aspects of management.

More than a decade later, the UKCC (2002) identified seven components of specialist practice in the publication of the higher level practice descriptors:

- providing effective healthcare
- research and evaluation
- developing self and others
- leading and developing practice
- working across professional and organizational boundaries
- innovation and changing practice
- improving quality and health outcomes.

These descriptors would seem to be broadly in line with earlier criteria developed in the USA from the literature. Research carried out by Castledine in 2003 identified core competencies to be found in the CNS, which also support the previous criteria. Castledine grouped the competencies under nine headings:

- direct clinical care
- improving quality and health outcomes
- evaluation and research
- teaching and educating others
- leading and developing practice
- innovation and changing practice
- scholarly activity, speaking, presenting, writing and publications
- developing self and others
- working across organizational boundaries.

The three sets of criteria outlined above are, in the main, in agreement regarding the components of specialist practice, and should facilitate the development of effective role descriptors and lead to more consistency in the use of the specialist title and clarity about the role. However, community healthcare services and hospital trusts continue to appoint individuals with a wide range of experience, education and ability to 'specialist' posts; this can lead to conflict and ambiguity regarding the specialist role (Castledine, 2004).

Glen and Waddington (1998) identified and discussed role conflict and role ambiguity, and suggested that these occur when there are differing views about the role and responsibilities and a lack of clarity regarding expectations. The role of the CNS has been subjected to a range of pressures from within the NHS (National Health Service and Community Care Act 1990), from recommendations from the UKCC (1991) and *The Scope of Professional Practice* (UKCC, 1992) and from recommendations on junior doctors' hours (NHS Management Executive [NHSME], 1991).

Additional demands were made in key policy documents related to cancer care, including *The Nursing Contribution to Cancer Care* (DH, 2000), *Cancer in Scotland: Action for Change* (Scottish Executive Health Department [SEHD], 2001a) and *Improving Health in Wales* (National Assembly for Wales, 2001). Further influences have been the *Agenda for Change* (DH, 2003a) and *The NHS Knowledge and Skills Framework* (DH, 2003b). The high demands of the role, both professionally and personally, add to the confusion sometimes experienced by those new to the specialist role, and pressure from a variety of sources can lead to difficulties in making the transition from generalist to specialist practitioner. Difficulties with transition can cause difficulties in adjusting to the role, often leading to individuals leaving prematurely or failing to function effectively at the level of specialist. Understanding how to facilitate role transition is a key element in developing effective specialist practitioners.

The psychology of transition

The notion of transition is not new, because life itself is a catalogue of changes. Some of the life changes are natural, eg. growing old, while others are necessary for survival, eg. educating oneself to better one's life. Other forms of change are beyond our control and are often externally driven. Such processes of transition seem to centre on the ability of the individual going through the change to remain in control or still exert some control over the situation itself. This is also a common desirable outcome in most people's everyday life in order for them to be effective in what they do (Covey, 1999).

The transition process in specialist practice tends to take place at different levels, such as physically moving from one job to another, moving from hospital to the community, or moving from being a member of a team to being a lone practitioner. There is also an attitude shift from a psychological point of view, where an individual makes a conscious decision to change his/her mental frame of reference when moving to a new or different role. Any transition is bound to provoke some psychological reaction. The success or failure of each transition depends on how the individual psychologically negotiates change from that which seems comfortable, familiar and was being practised with a degree of expertise, to an area that is relatively unfamiliar and requires a different set of skills. It would therefore seem logical to assume that transition needs to be facilitated and the individual making the transition needs to be supported both physically and psychologically. The transition from generic to specialist practice has an element of unfamiliarity, as an individual moves from what seems to be a comfort zone to a new territory of responsibility, and the key issue is how to manage this phase effectively.

The role of the specialist practitioner often comes without overt structures, boundaries or routines and requires the specialist practitioner to develop new ways of working; rigid routines become less important as the specialist practitioner assumes a more flexible and autonomous but interdependent way of working. Interdependent working involves a practitioner who can work independently first and then links with other professionals around him/her to achieve best practice.

Working in this way demands a change in the practitioner's mindset from that of starting and finishing work religiously at set times regardless of the needs of the service. Some specialist practitioners still find themselves guilt-ridden if they are not physically present in the office first thing in the morning. At specialist level it is important that such practitioners are not restricted by rules and rigid systems of working. What needs encouraging is working smarter and still being effective. For example, specialist practitioners should feel comfortable enough to work from home now and again where the role permits such practice, and this should be communicated to other staff and the line manager. This would seem sensible, as it is known that work offices are not always conducive to concentration or speaking privately to patients and relatives. In some organizations, with advanced technology, staff can still access work files and emails from home.

Role transition is an individual experience and its success or failure is very much dependent on three broad theories:

- **Psychological:** These focus on the thought process of the individual, which in turn help to place the transition into perspective. Here the meaning of the transition is brought into sharper focus and may be influenced by cultural values and norms.

- **Socio-emotional:** These focus on the affective aspect of the individual involved in the transition. The key considerations are relationships and how the change may affect these.

- **Behavioural:** These focus on the individual's overt observable behaviour while negotiating the change. It is important to stress that behaviour is the outcome of an interaction between psychological and emotional aspects of the individual. Positive behaviour manifested by an individual would suggest possible success in the transition, while the opposite is arguably true (Hopson and Adams, 1976; Nicholson, 1984).

In any transition, there are other drivers that are deemed intrinsic, eg. personal motivation, altruism in terms of doing good for others and personal achievement. External factors would include political, socio-economic, legal and technological factors, which the individual may have no control over. Hopson and Adams (1976) claim that during the transition phase, individuals may experience a fluctuation in their perception of their competence level. Hopson and Adams identified possible fluctuating points from the beginning of the transition to the point where the individual feels confident again in the new role (*Figure 4.1*).

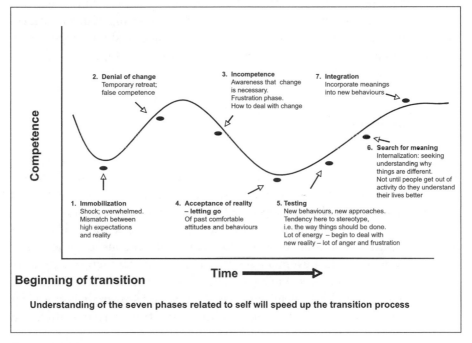

Figure 4.1: The transition curve

Although theorists such as Hopson and Adams consider this process normal in most transitions, there may not be any normality for the individual who is immersed in the transition. The feelings of immobilization (point 1 on *Figure 4.1*) may lead to complete denial of the change (point 2). The individual may also feel incompetent in this role; this is particularly difficult to rationalize for someone who may have been working at expert level in his/her previous role (see also the notion of regressive progression below).

What often happens is that, in a desperate attempt to survive in the new role, most individuals involved in transition tend not to let go of past comfortable attitudes and behaviours (point 4 on *Figure 4.1*). It can be argued that when this happens, such individuals often find themselves in a psychological 'no-man's land'. It is here that individuals may benefit from mentorship and practice-based facilitator (PBF) support. Such support is crucial to guiding the individual so that, with time, he/she may begin to feel competent again.

It is important to help those in transition to look for the opportunity value, which most outsiders can see but for them is elusive. Some of the skills learnt in previous roles can be used in the new job (transferable skills) but those in transition may not always remember that they have these skills; this is something that can be greatly facilitated with good mentorship or clinical supervision. Points 5–7 on *Figure 4.1* show steady progress towards functioning effectively and confidently in the new role. The individual will once again begin to feel in control and comfortable working at this new level of expertise. It is not yet clear how long on average it should take for an individual to negotiate this transition, and factors such as type and degree of support tend to play a crucial role in this.

Gains and losses

With each transition there are gains and losses. Gains often include perceptions of achievement, high status, improved remuneration, enhanced self-esteem and self-belief. Losses could be seen as psychological regression (see below), loss of familiarity, loss of confidence and a sense of novice-ness. Transition is a time of complex and simultaneous experiences – uncertainty, fear, joy, achievement, power, progression, feelings of insecurity and at times feelings of inadequacy (Bradby, 1990). What is at stake is how different people handle or deal with these gains and losses. It is not clear whether individuals consciously analyse the gains from any transition and compare them with the losses.

It could be argued that most people tend to focus on the negative aspects of change and somehow ignore the opportunity value in the same environment of change. A force-field analysis (after Lewin, 1951) of these two elements would be a useful exercise to perform. Lewin advocates an analysis based on factors that would support the change against those that work against it. The importance of such analysis is that the individual will be better prepared to pre-empt or minimize the negative forces and still have a successful transition. Nicholson (1984) has argued, among other points, that if the transition is a planned one, as opposed to being imposed, it is logical to suggest that the gains would outweigh the losses. However, what is crucial is the mode of adjustment that individuals adopt to avoid transition itself becoming a source of stress (Brett, 1980).

Another point to consider is the perception that the individual brings to this transition in terms of gains and losses. How individuals perceive different things and their approach to life in general can influence the experience of transition. For example, metaphorically speaking, some people tend to see a half-full glass of water (positive outlook) while others see the same glass as half-empty (negative outlook); it is possible that these individuals will also bring their particular outlook into the transition process. Nicholson (1984) describes this in a more technical language, and considers the psychological disposition and motives of the individual engaged in role transition. Nicholson argues that the end-result of any transition is achieving stability of the individual and the situation around him/her. This is where mentors and PBFs can play a crucial role in helping and guiding individuals to recognize their perceptions and then move to a different (preferably positive) mindset, which focuses on identifying the opportunity within and the value of each transition. In other words, the whole process of integrating the new person into new roles (organizational socialization) is central to how that individual will adjust to the new challenges.

We also have to accept that some individuals may not be able to seize the opportunity and their perceptions will therefore remain negatively entrenched, to the extent that sickness and absenteeism become common or, alternatively, securing another job becomes the only viable option. This option should be the last resort in such a process. However, when supporting individuals through transition it is also important to consider their prior experiences (if any) and how they may have negotiated these. Nicholson calls this prior occupational socialization; if it was painful, then the current transition may serve as a reminder of that experience. For more detailed discussion of work role transition, the reader is referred to the work of Nicholson (1984).

The notion of regressive progression

It is important to recognize and acknowledge that although progress (moving to a specialist level) is being made, individuals operate psychologically on the premise that they are in fact regressing to unfamiliar territory without the skills, knowledge and competencies expected at the new level (Hopson and Adams, 1976; Westen, 1996). It is not until the new skills, attitudes and behaviours required or expected at this new level are mastered that progression is eventually recognized, hence the regressive progression phenomenon. The time required for this psychological shift varies; Bradby (1990) found that student nurses needed 6–10 months post-qualification to begin to function fully as a trained nurse. Hamric and Taylor (1989) identified the development stages to specialist practice and suggested that this may take 3–5 years. Lack of a specific time frame may reflect the complexity of this emotional process, which in turn suggests that individual differences exist in the pace of negotiating the transition.

According to Hamric and Taylor (1989), different researchers (Baker, 1979; Baker, 1987; Kramer, 1974; Oda, 1977) have identified up to four phases of role development to specialist practice. The phases all start from a position of relative insecurity to an endpoint of competence and confidence (Hamric and Spross, 1989). This complexity may explain why role transition is often associated with individuals not 'letting go' of old practices (see *Figure 4.1*), which in these circumstances would provide a comfort zone. It is often surprising how individuals in a transition forget to utilize those transferable skills acquired in their previous roles. If skills were transferred, the perception of regressive progression would simultaneously be minimized.

Glen and Waddington (1998), whose work was influenced by Nicholson's (1984) model of work role transitions, identified six key factors that needed to be in place to facilitate role transition from generalist to specialist practice. Factors that impeded transition included the absence of any of these key factors and a resistance to change on the part of either the individual or the organization. The key factors were:

- a need for induction into and preparation for the role, including professional, clinical and organizational aspects of the role, time management and stress management
- clear role definitions and boundaries
- effective interprofessional relationships
- appraisal and supervision
- a support network of specialist practitioners
- a clearly articulated career pathway and professional development for the role of the specialist practitioner.

It has been acknowledged that nurses at all levels, who take on new roles, require adequate preparation to facilitate the transition from generalist to specialist practitioner (Shewan and Read, 1999). The problems inherent in making that transition, together with the ambiguity and confusion that often surround specialist practitioner roles, suggest that the provision of adequate preparation and support is crucial to the development of specialist practitioners and subsequently specialist practice.

Preparation for specialist roles

Historically, CNSs have been appointed with little or no preparation for the role; as a result, although they may have highly developed clinical skills they appear to struggle with the other components of the specialist role discussed earlier in this chapter. In the past decade, a number of academic courses for the cancer and palliative care practitioner have been developed, at both level 3 and master's level. Practitioners aspiring to the specialist role are encouraged to study to a minimum of level 3 and ideally go on to study at master's level (UKCC, 2002). There is now more opportunity to undertake a range of academic courses in specialist areas and many nurses undertake higher degrees relatively soon after registration.

This has resulted in the appointment to specialist posts of practitioners who have the relevant academic qualifications but may not have sufficient clinical experience in the specialty or may not have had the experience of working at a more senior level. Equally, there are those who may have a lot of direct clinical experience but lack the confidence and skills to develop the components of specialist practice discussed earlier. This inability to fully develop the specialist role may result in avoidance of key aspects of the role, job dissatisfaction, burnout and a failure to impact effectively on the delivery of effective health care and service development at a specialist level (Glen and Waddington, 1998).

In order to address these issues in the development of its specialist practitioners, Macmillan Cancer Relief developed the Macmillan Role Development Programme (MRDP). This four-module work-based learning programme was developed specifically to facilitate the transition from generalist to specialist practitioner and support the practitioner in developing the knowledge, skills and confidence necessary to fully undertake the role of specialist practitioner in cancer and palliative care. The work-based learning model is supported by the support mechanisms, which are integral to the programme, and the use of learning contracts as the method of assessment. Both aspects of the programme will be discussed later in this chapter.

The programme evolved from a successful pilot project undertaken by Macmillan Cancer Relief from 1998 to 2000. Following a positive evaluation (Beech, 2001) a decision was made to take forward the development of a programme that would meet the needs of new specialist practitioners in cancer and palliative care. The programme was developed initially from the literature and *A Higher Level of Practice* (UKCC, 1999a), and was subsequently cross-referenced to the relevant health-related publications across the four nations. These included:

- *Cancer in Scotland: Action for Change* (SEHD, 2001a)
- *The Nursing Contribution to Cancer Care* (DH, 2000)
- *Report of the Higher Level of Practice Pilot and Project.* (UKCC, 2002)
- *Draft Code of Practice for the Assurance of Academic Quality and Standards in Higher Education: Section 9, Placement learning* (Quality Assurance Agency, 2001)
- *Fitness for Practice* (UKCC, 1999b)
- *Standards for the Preparation of Teachers of Nursing, Midwifery and Health Visiting* (UKCC, 2000a).

Latterly the learning outcomes have been reviewed, taking into account the *Knowledge and Skills Framework* (DH, 2003b) and *Agenda for Change* (DH, 2003a). The programme was underpinned by the following principles:

- A supportive environment will enhance the individual's learning potential.
- The teaching and assessment methods will allow the individual to explore his/her own learning needs within the context of his/her own practice and support lifelong learning.
- A work-based learning approach will facilitate the application of theory to practice.
- A structured programme of learning and development supported in practice will facilitate the transition from generalist to specialist.

Role development programme and structure

The programme is divided into four 12-week modules, which address the key components of the specialist role as identified in the literature and in the aforementioned documents. Each module contains a theory component (4 days) and a practice component (11 weeks) and addresses a different aspect of the specialist role, allowing the practitioner to explore areas relevant to his/her own practice.

The overall aim of the programme is to enable the individual to develop the necessary skills to function as a specialist practitioner, take an active and leading role in the delivery, development and improvement of cancer and palliative care services, and apply higher levels of enquiry, reflective and evaluation skills to facilitate his/her continuing professional development.

Module 1: Working effectively in specialist practice

This module aims to enable the learner to utilize a range of strategies appropriately in order to begin working autonomously and as a member of the multiprofessional team. It addresses some of the key areas necessary for effective working at specialist level, including role boundaries, multidisciplinary working, effective team-working and clinical decision-making. These topics are integral to the role of the specialist practitioner and central to the process of working with others for the benefit of patient care. Expertise in making clinical decisions is one of the hallmarks of advanced practice, and specialist practitioners are required to make clinical judgments, for which they are both responsible and accountable, every day in their clinical practice. These judgments and decisions are dependent on the practitioner's ability to attend to and process relevant data from both the clinical situation and information from professional colleagues.

The module also allows the practitioner to explore the nature of the therapeutic relationship and the development of strategies and resources necessary for successful personal management in the specialist role.

Module 2: Governance in specialist practice

Module 2 focuses on governance issues such as quality assurance, risk management and audit, enabling the practitioner to develop the skills, knowledge and confidence necessary to evaluate the clinical effectiveness of the service that he/she delivers. The practitioner is encouraged to develop an understanding of the key issues in quality assurance in clinical practice, and to explore the range of mechanisms available for evaluating the structure process and outcome of cancer and palliative care services. The module also explores the role of evidence-based practice in ensuring quality care and enables the practitioner to compare and contrast audit and research processes within the context of quality assurance in clinical care.

Module 3: The role of specialist practitioners in facilitating learning

Teaching and learning are central components of specialist practice in cancer and palliative care, both in the context of the practitioner's own continuing professional development and the development of others. Specialist practitioners are often called on to provide education for a range of professionals, although few of them have had any formal preparation. Module 3 allows them to explore different ways of approaching education both formally and informally. The module includes sessions on information provision, teaching methods, evaluation and planning and preparing for teaching in a variety of settings. This enables practitioners to extend their knowledge, skills and expertise in facilitating learning, so that they can respond confidently to a range of teaching and learning situations.

Module 4: Managing and leading in specialist practice

Module 4 brings together all the elements of the first three modules and allows the practitioner to explore the attributes required to function fully as a specialist practitioner and to develop the confidence to undertake a leadership role. Practitioners are encouraged to explore their own leadership and management styles within the context of their clinical practice. They are also introduced to the political imperatives influencing the delivery of cancer and palliative care services at both national and local levels. They are able to consider recent significant reviews of service delivery and the recommendations and policies that have resulted from these. Other areas addressed within the module include strategic planning, business planning, report writing and implementing change.

Assessment

Learning contracts form the principal method of assessment of the MRDP. They bridge the theory–practice gap by translating theoretical knowledge into practice-based knowledge and behaviour. They are developed by the learner and allow him/her to identify and meet his/her own learning needs within the context of each module (Knowles, 1986). This allows the learner a measure of control over his/her own learning and development, guided by the PBF and the academic supervisor. The principle of the learning contract is to formulate an agreement between the learner, the PBF and the academic supervisor about the intended nature of the learning. The learning contract becomes similar to an action plan or a self-development plan and should consider the following questions (Knowles, 1986):

- What do I need to learn?
- What strategies and resources do I need to employ?
- What evidence can I provide to demonstrate that I have learned?
- How will I prove that I have learned it?

Learning contracts provide a way of defining areas to explore within the scope of each module as they relate to areas of practice. They also have an important role to play in learning how to learn, eg. they help the practitioner to:

- specify learning goals and establish criteria for success and achievement
- improve diagnostic, decision-making and self-development abilities
- increase the personal relevance, motivation and self-direction in learning
- be more systematic when reflecting on individual learning styles.

Some examples of what was achieved through the learning contracts are illustrated below:

Module 1   The development of steroid therapy guidelines for patients discharged to the community

Module 2   An audit resulting in an improvement in access to an out-of-hours palliative care drug service in a remote rural area

Module 3   Development and delivery of a cancer/palliative care education programme for non-specialist hospital nurses

Module 4   Development and implementation of a trust-wide strategy for the management of syringe drivers

Support

Although this section appears at the end of the chapter, it is by no means the least important aspect of the programme, and in reality is one of its most important components. The quality of support in the clinical learning environment has been identified as critical for the success of a work-based learning programme. The need for high-quality clinical experience to support the acquisition of clinical skills has also been recognized in the literature (Dearing Report, 1997; Flanagan *et al*, 2000; QAA, 2001; UKCC, 1999b, 2000b). Each learner on the MRDP worked closely with a senior clinical practitioner, who acted as a PBF, facilitating the application of theory to clinical practice for the learner while supporting other aspects of his/her development. Key responsibilities of the PBF include directing some of the learning activities in support of learning, providing feedback, providing help and support with learning contracts and sharing clinical knowledge and expertise.

The PBFs attend a 3-day training workshop developed by the Macmillan National Insitute of Education (MNIE) in order to prepare for the role. In this workshop they are able to explore their own feelings and experiences of the specialist role as well as developing skills in facilitating learning. This is a challenging role to undertake, and adequate support for those undertaking it is vital. They need to have access to the course leader and/or academic supervisor and should be encouraged to support one another in the role. Where distance is not an obstacle they can meet regularly, or if distances are too great they can be encouraged to form an email supportive network.

Evaluation

The programme was evaluated throughout and the evaluation process included key stakeholders, such as clinical managers, as well as the course participants. The evaluations were carried out using a combination of pre- and post-module self-report questionnaires, which measured confidence in their ability and skills and understanding of the course content, and module satisfaction questionnaires. The results demonstrated a significant increase in levels of both confidence and understanding across most measures in each module, suggesting that practitioners felt better able to function at specialist level. Satisfaction questionnaires indicated a high degree of satisfaction with the programme. 'Impact on practice' questionnaires were sent to key stakeholders; the results showed that there was a discernible increase in the ability and confidence of practitioners.

Overall, the evaluation demonstrated that the MRDP positively influences the development of specialist nurses, bridging the theory–practice gap, enabling nurses to improve and develop areas of clinical practice. The evaluation results were presented at the International Cancer Nurses Conference 2004 and the *Nurse Education Today* 2005 Conference, and a paper is currently being prepared for publication.

Summary

The MRDP is an evidence-based programme designed to enable practitioners to undertake the complex role of specialist practitioner. The curriculum addresses the range of knowledge and skills necessary to practise at specialist level, and the assessment process and support mechanisms make it easier for the practitioner to develop confidence in the role. This combination has been a key factor in achieving the aims of the programme. The programme takes cognisance of the literature and relevant professional and political documents regarding specialist practice, guiding learners to successful transition, as identified by Glen and Waddington (1998), through the combination of teaching, work-based assessment, learning and professional support in the clinical area.

Feedback from the MRDP has been consistently positive, and anecdotal evidence from learners who have undertaken the programme suggests that it has achieved its aims:

> *"I have better understanding of the role of the specialist practitioner." "It's the first time I have been really able to see the application of theory to practice." "It enables me to look at areas that are relevant to improving patient care."*

The following two case studies present a more personal view of how the MRDP enabled the development of each learner. All names have been changed to ensure anonymity. In the second case study, both Laura and her PBF give personal accounts of their experience of the role development programme.

Facilitating and supporting role transition – two case studies

Case study – Jane

Jane is an experienced district nurse with a community nursing degree with Specialist Practitioner Award, whose career pathway was focused on working as a community palliative care nurse. The opportunity for moving into this role arose through her successful application to a Macmillan CNS development post with the requirement to attend and successfully complete the MRDP. Her immediate concerns were that some elements of the programme would be a repetition of aspects of the Specialist Practitioner Award, as close scrutiny of the MRDP module outcomes reflected the core elements of specialist practice.

Her second concern was the nature of the assessment process. Work-based learning was not familiar to her and she was unsure of the concomitant work commitment combined with the challenges of starting and coming to terms

cont./..

with her new role. Her third concern was commuting backwards and forwards to the university to undertake the modules. Jane found that the modules of the MRDP did have elements of repetition; however, because of the practical focus of the teaching and assessment she was able to consolidate previous learning and apply this to practice.

Both modules 1 and 2 ('Working Effectively in Clinical Practice' and 'Research and Quality in Clinical Practice') enabled Jane to undertake work in practice that would have a direct and indirect impact on patient care. For example, she developed a patient medication chart for patients in the community, which enabled patients, carers and community professionals to see at a glance which medications were prescribed and why. This in turn provided opportunities to discuss symptom management as a means of information giving. This was described as not just a paper exercise, but also something that is still being used successfully within the community. Jane also developed an audit form that enabled the team to audit their notes, thereby contributing to the governance agenda.

The 'Teaching and Learning' module gave Jane the opportunity to put teaching principles into practice in both the classroom and her practice area. Gaining skills in PowerPoint presentation and planning and preparing for teaching increased her confidence, and the module provided the opportunity to develop these in context. Accessing a short programme around presentation skills was not an option at the time of doing the programme and would have required additional study time. Module 4 ('Managing and Leading Specialist Practice') brought the individual components together, enabling her to see how all the elements of the role were necessary in order to influence patient care either directly or indirectly, even if the immediate impact on the patient could not be measured.

Jane felt that it was important to undertake the entire programme to see the full benefits. Although work-based learning was a new concept for her, Jane felt that it was suitable for her reflective learning style and enabled her to pace herself while adjusting to a new role. Selecting her own learning outcomes provided meaning to the experience, and motivation when change occurred. The latter was important because at times both she and her colleagues were tired. Spin-offs to the work-based learning were the opportunities to work closely with her colleagues, particularly her PBF, and having to network in order to meet work-based learning outcomes. Both of these assisted in facilitating her transition to her new role.

The MRDP gave Jane the opportunities to meet with CNSs from other parts of the country and provided an informal support system that would continue after she had completed the course. The programme also allowed Jane to reflect on the practice of others – an opportunity that would not have been available had she attended a local course where all the participants had come from the same location.

Despite the hard work, Jane feels that the programme offered what was needed at that time of role transition in terms of support, appropriate content and the opportunity to see the fruits of her labour in practice.

Case study: Laura

Two years ago, I was fortunate to be appointed to a Macmillan CNS development post within a large teaching hospital and cancer centre. Although I had previously studied at level 3 and was well experienced, having worked for 15 years in the health service, I vividly remember my first few months in the new role.

I felt totally overwhelmed and anxious about my performance. I missed the camaraderie of ward work and feeling part of a team. My 'new' team (two other CNSs and a consultant) seemed very knowledgeable and confident and were well known and accepted throughout the hospital.

As part of my development I was asked to undertake the MRDP. As module 1 was about 'Working Effectively in Specialist Practice', it seemed very relevant to my needs. I will describe key aspects of the programme that worked for me.

The structure of the module was as follows:

- four days' intensive teaching and learning (away from clinical caseload)
- support and networking with peers (in the same boat)
- eleven weeks to undertake practice-based learning on aspects of clinical practice that I identified
- encouragement to contact my academic supervisor and submit draft learning contract.

Although I found the concept of the learning contract very hard to grasp, once I started to work on my objectives and put together a plan of how I could meet them, I began to see how this could really help me organize my work

cont./..

and positively influence the care of patients referred. It was hard and time consuming, but very rewarding, to complete my learning contract, especially since the whole team took on board the importance of clear referral criteria for the service.

My relationship with my PBF comprised the following:

- initial meeting to set the ground rules
- monthly meetings for support and to check progress
- time to debrief and reflect on what was going well
- appropriate challenge to improve practice and understand team dynamics
- observation of my practice.

This was a totally new experience for me. It took a while to build trust as I was in awe of my facilitator's knowledge and breadth of experience in the field. He was very honest and reassured me that the feelings I had were common and to be expected when working in a new role. He helped me to meet my learning outcomes by encouraging me to be more realistic and specific about what I needed to do. One particular challenge for me was a session on observed practice, when my PBF came to watch how I admitted patients to the service and discharged them. I was very nervous initially, as I had no previous experience of this; however, as we planned this rigorously and I asked for the type of feedback I required, this was a very positive learning experience. In particular, it helped me realize how to manage future occasions when I was accompanied by staff wishing to shadow me in my role. Also, I realized that I now expect any visitor to the team to set their objectives for the visit.

In summary, my confidence has grown over the past 9 months, partly from working in clinical practice and receiving feedback from patients, colleagues and PBF, but also from feeling confident directly as a result of undertaking this module. I have developed my own network of support and some strategies for coping with the demands of the role. I feel that I am beginning to have a place within the team and that I am much more aware of the specialist role and boundaries of that role.

Experience of Laura's practice-based facilitator

I had misgivings when I met Laura for the first time. My impression was that she was very tearful and lacking in confidence. She had had a previous bad experience of academic learning and was apprehensive about how she would manage the coursework as well as fitting into a new team. Although a very experienced and competent practitioner, she described feeling de-skilled and out of her comfort zone in her new role. I wondered how she would cope with the pressures of work and study.

We set ground rules and I shared some of my thoughts and feelings when I started as a CNS. I asked Laura to highlight some of her positive attributes and to reflect on why she had applied for, and been successful in getting, this development post. By the end I felt that Laura had relaxed a little; we arranged to meet the following week and then at monthly intervals. I tried to reassure her that this was a *development* post and that transition into a new role is a process.

Over the past few months I have been very impressed with Laura's determination and commitment to her development. It has not been easy but she has worked hard to reach her objectives and is growing in confidence and self-belief. I have learned a lot from her and from the process of facilitating her development. After the module we reflected together on what it means to be a specialist and had some challenging discussion and debates around the role. I was also struck by the positive influence that Laura's development has had on her team, as it has made them scrutinize, reflect and evaluate aspects of their own practice.

Vision for the future

The MRDP has proved to be an effective mechanism for supporting new specialist practitioners in their role transition. As an established yet dynamic role, specialist practice will continue to respond to healthcare policies and developments, hence the need for constructive support for new specialists will continue. The MRDP, with its clear work-based focus and clinical support systems, must be flexible and responsive in order to continue to meet the needs of specialist practitioners. Changes will initially occur in practice, and educational institutes need to keep abreast of these and provide appropriate programmes. The continued evolution of clinical specialist practice and advanced practice necessitates a focus on work-based learning to enable development of the roles in the light of clinical demands and challenges. This is where the strength of the MRDP lies; this focus must be maintained, independent of how the programme evolves within the education institutions and the academic level at which the MRDP is offered.

Any new role associated with specialist or advanced practice will, by its nature, comprise a period of transition during which practitioners require support and the facilitation of skills and knowledge development. Any programme purporting to provide this support and facilitation must retain the clinical focus, promoting work-based learning in order to offer an educational programme that is real and relevant to the practitioner's clinical needs. The emphasis of the MRDP on the application to practice, with provision of relevant underlying theories, will enable practitioners to be supported in practice as they continue to develop into their new roles, making appropriate changes in practice, and to become assimilated into their teams more readily.

References

Baker PO (1987) Model activities for clinical nurse specialist role development. *Clin Nurse Spec* **1**(3): 119–23

Baker V (1979) Retrospective explorations in role development. In: Padilla GV (ed) *The Clinical Nurse Specialist and Improvement of Nursing Practice*. Wakefield, MA: 56–63

Bamford O, Gibson F (2000) The clinical nurse specialist: perceptions of practising CNSs of their role and development needs. *J Clin Nurs* **9**: 282–92

Beech N (2001) Evaluation of the pilot training scheme. Department of Education, Macmillan Cancer Relief, London

Benner P (1984) *From Novice to Expert: Excellence and power in clinical nursing practice*. Addison-Wesley, Menlo Park, California

Bousfield C (1997) A phenomenological investigation into the role of the clinical nurse specialist. *J Adv Nurs* **25**(2): 245–56

Bradby M (1990) Status passage into nursing: another view of the process of socialization into nursing. *J Adv Nurs* **15**(10): 1220–5

Brett JM (1980) The effect of job transfer on employees and their families. In: Cooper CL, Payne R (eds) *Current Concerns in Occupational Stress*. Wiley, Chichester: 99–136

Burwell CG (1989) Clinical experience for the clinical nurse specialist. Unpublished thesis. Teachers College, Columbia University, Columbia

Castledine G (1982) The role and functions of clinical nurse specialists in England and Wales. Unpublished MSc thesis. University of Manchester, England

Castledine G (2003) Report of research conducted at Shrewsbury and Telford NHS Hospital Trust. In: McGee P, Castledine G (eds) *Advanced Nursing Practice*. 2nd edn. Blackwell Publishing, Oxford

Castledine G (2004) Generalist and specialist nurses – complementary or conflicting roles? In: *New Nursing Roles: Deciding the Future for Scotland*. Scottish Executive Health Department, Edinburgh

Covey SR (1999) *The Seven Habits of Highly Effective People.* Simon & Schuster UK Ltd, London

Daly WM, Carnwell R (2003) Nursing roles and levels of practice: a framework for differentiating between elementary, specialist and advancing nursing practice. *J Clin Nurs* **12**(2): 158–67

Dearing Report (1997) *Higher Education in the Learning Society. Report of the National Committee of Inquiry into Higher Education.* HMSO, London

Department of Health (2000) *The Nursing Contribution to Cancer Care: A strategic programme of action in support of the National Cancer Programme.* DH, London

Department of Health (2003a) *Agenda for Change.* DH, London

Department of Health (2003b) *The NHS Knowledge and Skills Framework and Related Development Review.* DH, London

Flanagan J, Baldwin S, Clarke D (2000) Work-based learning as a means of developing and assessing nursing competence. *J Clin Nurs* **9**(3): 360–8

Girard N (1987) The CNS: development of the role. In: Menard S (ed) *The Clinical Nurse Specialist: Perspectives on practice.* John Wiley, New York: 9–33

Glen S, Waddington K (1998) Role transition from staff nurse to clinical nurse specialist: a case study. *J Clin Nurs* **7**(3): 283–90

Hamric BA, Spross JA (eds) (1989) *The Clinical Nurse Specialist in Theory and Practice.* 2nd edn. WB Saunders, Philadelphia

Hamric BA, Taylor JW (1989) Role development of the CNS. In: Hamric BA, Spross JA (eds) *The Clinical Nurse Specialist in Theory and Practice.* 2nd edn. WB Saunders, Philadelphia

Hopson B, Adams J (1976) Towards an understanding of transitions: defining some boundaries of transition dynamics. In: Adams J, Hayes J, Hopson B (eds) *Transition: Understanding and Managing Personal Change.* Martin Robertson, London

Jack B, Oldham J, Williams A (2003) A stakeholder evaluation of the impact of the palliative care clinical nurse specialist upon doctors and nurses within an acute hospital setting. *Palliat Med* **17**(3): 283–8

Knowles M (1986) *Using Learning Contracts.* Jossey-Bass, San Francisco

Kramer M (1974) *Reality Shock – Why Nurses Leave Nursing.* CV Mosby, St Louis

Lewin K (1951) *Field Theory in Social Science.* Harper Row, New York

Loudermilk L (1990) Role ambiguity and the clinical nurse specialist. *Nursingconnections* **3**(1): 3–12

McGee P, Castledine G, Brown R (1996) A survey of specialist and advanced nursing practice in England. *Br J Nurs* **5**(11): 682–6

Montemuro M (1987) The evolution of the clinical nurse specialist: response to the challenge of professional nursing practice. *Clin Nurse Spec* **1**(3): 106–10

National Assembly for Wales (2001) *Improving Health in Wales: A plan for the NHS with its partners.* NafW, Cardiff

NHS Management Executive (1991) *Junior Doctors: The New Deal.* HMSO, London

Nicholson N (1984) A theory of work role transitions. *Adm Sci Q* 29: 172–91

NMC (2005) *Consultation on a Framework for the Standard for Post-registration Nursing.* NMC, London

Oda D (1977) Specialised role development: a three-phase process. *Nurs Outlook* **25:** 374–7

Quality Assurance Agency (2001) *Draft Code of Practice for the Assurance of Academic Quality and Standards in Higher Education: Section 9, Placement learning.* QAA, Gloucester

RCN (1974) *The State of Nursing.* RCN Publications, London

RCN (1981a) *A Structure for Nursing.* RCN Publications, London

RCN (1981b) *Standards of Nursing Care.* RCN Publications, London

Redekopp MA (1997) Clinical nurse specialist role confusion: the need for identity. *Clinical Nurse Specialist* **11**(2): 87–91

Redmond K (2000) Clinical decision making. In: Kearney N, Richardson A, Di Giulio P (eds) *Cancer Nursing Practice: A textbook for the specialist nurse.* Churchill Livingstone, Edinburgh: 61–89

Reiter F (1966) The nurse clinician. *Am J Nurs* **66**(2): 274–80

Scottish Executive Health Department (2001a) *Cancer in Scotland: Action for Change.* SEHD, Edinburgh

Scottish Executive Health Department (2001b) *Facing the Future. Report of the 19 November 2001 Convention on Recruitment and Retention in Nursing and Midwifery.* SEHD, Edinburgh

Seymour J, Clark D, Hughes P *et al* (2002) Clinical nurse specialists in palliative care. Part 3: Issues for the Macmillan nurse role. *Palliat Med* **16**(5): 386–94

Shewan JA, Read SM (1999) Changing roles in nursing: a literature review of influences and innovations. *Clinical Effectiveness in Nursing* **3:** 75–82

Skilbeck J, Corner J, Bath P *et al* (2002) Clinical nurse specialists in palliative care. Part 1: A description of the Macmillan nurse caseload. *Palliat Med* **16**(4): 285–96

Tackenberg JN, Rausch AM (1995) Redefining the role of clinical nurse specialists. *Adv Pract Nurs Q* **1**(1): 37–48

UKCC (1991) *Post-Registration Education and Practice Project.* UKCC, London

UKCC (1992) *The Scope of Professional Practice.* UKCC, London

UKCC (1999a) *A Higher Level of Practice. Report of the consultation on the UKCC's proposal for a revised regulatory framework for post-registration clinical practice.* UKCC, London

UKCC (1999b) *Fitness for Practice.* The UKCC Commission for Nursing and Midwifery Education. Chair: Sir Leonard Peach. UKCC, London

UKCC (2000a) *Standards for the Preparation of Teachers of Nursing, Midwifery and Health Visiting.* UKCC, London

UKCC (2000b) *Fitness for Practice and Purpose. Report of the UKCC's Post Commission Development Group.* UKCC, London

UKCC (2002) *Report of the Higher Level of Practice Pilot and Project.* UKCC, London

Westen D (1996) *Psychology: Mind, brain and culture.* John Wiley and Son, New York

Woods L (1998) Implementing advanced practice: identifying the factors that facilitate and inhibit the process. *J Clin Nurs* **7**(3): 265–73

CHAPTER 5

What is succession planning and how can it be made to work?

Nic Hughes, Catherine Jack

In this chapter, we define 'succession planning', review and critique the literature on succession planning and propose a framework for understanding key concepts and processes. Some recent and current initiatives for making succession planning work are also outlined. We use Covey's idea of the 'circle of concern' (Covey, 1999) to represent our main focus, which is the specialist workforce in cancer and palliative care in the UK.

Introduction

What is succession planning? At a basic level the phrase 'succession planning' clearly refers to 'planning for something that is to follow'; however, this begs the question 'planning for what to follow what?' In the context of this book, succession planning means putting plans in place to ensure a stable and continually renewed workforce of specialists in cancer and palliative care (nurses, doctors, allied health professionals [AHPs]). In particular, it means developing people to enable them to take up key leadership positions, otherwise the phrase is indistinguishable from 'workforce planning'– an equally important, related but different activity. And who does the planning? According to the literature, it is the responsibility of managers and leaders to develop, write and communicate a succession plan as part of the strategic plan for their organization.

Literature search

A keyword search of PubMed using the phrase 'succession planning' identified 101 articles appearing between 1987 and 2003. If the words 'succession' or 'succession planning' appeared in the title, the article was retrieved. Additionally, if the abstract suggested that the article would be relevant to the theme of succession planning, then the article was retrieved. On this basis, 45 articles were retrieved and reviewed. Of these, 31 were directly relevant to succession planning; the remainder covered a range of management and organizational themes. With one exception, these articles were by North American authors and appeared in North American journals. A further search was made of the *Cumulated Index to Nursing and Allied Health Literature* (CINAHL) with the aim of identifying a British health-related literature on the subject. This keyword search yielded 26 articles, 19 of which had been identified in the PubMed search; only one of these was British, and had also been identified in the PubMed search.

Literature review

A review of these 31 articles revealed that they were all written with a focus on health care from a perspective of health care as a business. Many were written from a perspective of human resource management. Different healthcare environments were represented (acute hospital, home care, long-term care) and the same messages about succession planning appeared repeatedly. According to this consensus, succession planning has a number of key features:

- It is essential for any enterprise to survive and grow in a changing environment.
- It is a management responsibility.
- It is often neglected.
- It is difficult but not impossible.
- It needs investment of time and money.

In most of these articles the emphasis is on succession planning to replace senior executive managers, although many of the authors stress the importance of managing transitions to key roles in the organization at all levels. Some refer specifically to nurses or physicians, but most refer more broadly to healthcare leadership. Interestingly, most recommend the identification of internal talent before looking for external candidates, except in small numbers to bring in fresh perspectives. Recommended reasons for designing and implementing a succession planning strategy are uniform, as are most of the methods to be used. There are some differences of focus, ranging from identifying specific individuals and grooming them as a successor (Pulce, 2002) to creating an 'acceleration pool' (Byham and Nelson, 1999) as a tool for developing a larger number of individuals who may or may not eventually gain promotion. Although promotion is rarely guaranteed under such a scheme of accelerated development, there are said to be other benefits both to the individual and to the organization. At the other end of this continuum, broad development opportunities are offered which may lead to individuals gaining leadership roles in other organizations. It is noteworthy that only one article specifically refers to this, and regards it not as a failure of retention but as a success for succession planning more generally (Hope-Smeltzer, 2002).

All these papers are authored by people with experience in the field as nurse or physician managers or as chief executive officers (CEOs) or management consultants. There is little research base cited beyond the occasional employer survey, and almost no reference to related literature. Bower (2000) is a notable exception, offering a model for developing succession planning based on vision, networking and mentoring, which is supported by reference to a wide range of literature.

It is clear from reviewing this body of literature that there is overlap between the concept of succession planning as a management tool that involves grooming one or more individuals to take over specific senior roles in an organization, and that of more general leadership and workforce development.

Defining succession planning

Many of the articles reviewed offer a definition of succession planning. Some place an emphasis on filling key positions in an organization. Thus, according to Pulce (2002), succession planning is:

'A process by which one or more successors are identified for key positions and can be mentored and readily prepared to step into those jobs.'

Soares (2002) concurs with this, suggesting that it is:

'An ongoing process of systematically identifying, assessing and developing talent to ensure the leadership continuity for key positions in an organization.'

Smith (2002) approaches succession planning in the same way, describing it as:

'A defined program that an organization systematizes to ensure leadership continuity for all key positions by developing activities that will build personnel talent from within.'

Smith goes on to suggest, however, that:

'There is a need for more than simply a replacement strategy. At the heart of a solid succession plan is leadership development.'

This argument is spelled out in more detail by Hope-Smeltzer (2002), elaborating on her view that:

'Succession planning is not solely for the purpose of filling your (i.e. CEO) position in the future. With gaps in leadership and leadership development being a major challenge in healthcare, succession planning needs to be viewed more broadly ... [It] means preparing individuals for future roles, not just positions in your institution.'

Fruth (2003) echoes this view with her belief that succession planning is important at all levels of clinical care, not just higher management. She suggests that:

'Succession planning needs to begin with first-line managers and continue across nursing leadership's continuum'.

In a long paper which argues that succession planning depends for its success on relationship management, Tahan (2002) defines succession planning as a:

'... strategic decision-making and visioning process applied by leaders to ensure the presence of leadership and availability of leaders for the future.'

Tahan is blunt in emphasizing that succession planning must occur at all levels of the organization if it is to be effective, and adds, importantly, that:

'The succession plan must be made available in writing as a special part of the strategic plan.'

Finally, recording experience from the legal field that is transferable to health care, Woodhouse (2002) presents succession planning as a strategy for growing a new set of professionals, not just grooming for specific roles.

Following this overview of the literature we offer a conceptual framework that incorporates key aspects of succession planning described in the literature, and analyse current initiatives in specialist cancer and palliative care in the UK in the light of that framework.

The overarching idea in the literature is that succession planning is both a professional and an ethical obligation, whether the dominant approach is to ensure a replacement for a key position in a single organization or to develop a pool of talented individuals who may take up leadership roles across a range of organizations. *Figure 5.1* indicates some central themes and processes underpinning these approaches to succession planning.

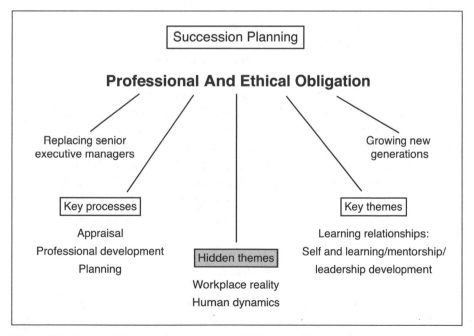

Figure 5.1: Succession planning conceptual framework

Key processes

Key processes that have been identified as facilitating effective succession planning include staff appraisal systems, provision of professional development and strategic planning. Staff appraisal can be used to identify existing levels of knowledge and skills in the workforce and to nurture the growth and potential of talented individuals. A wide range of professional development activities should be accessible, including work-based learning, open and distance learning, and further and higher education, all leading to relevant professional qualifications. Strategic planning is a central part of the succession planning process. Strategic plans should be clearly written in consultation with the workforce and other stakeholders (see www.leeds.ac.uk/strategy for a good example). In reality, strategic succession planning does not often receive the investment of time and resources that it merits in the modern workplace.

Key themes

Key themes that are central to making these processes effective include learning relationships, learning and innovation and leadership development. There is a diverse range of learning relationships in the modern workplace, including supervision, coaching, mentoring and networking. These relationships have received increasing amounts of attention in recent years and are often formalized. They are used to help practitioners achieve optimum performance in their role and also to prepare for career progression. These one-to-one learning relationships can have a high impact in accelerating growth and development. Learning relationships should be coupled with learning projects to stimulate and stretch the individual. A diverse range of learning activities at all levels will not only foster personal and professional growth and development but may also enhance performance and the generation of new ideas (Smith, 2002).

In contemporary thinking about leadership, there has been a shift away from emphasizing innate traits for leadership towards an understanding that leadership skills can be learned. For example, competent and creative leaders need to be able to (Corso, 2002):

- scan information quickly (noticing)
- create understanding (sense making)
- positively connect with inner drives and interests (personalizing)
- create an environment respectful of feelings and intuition (legitimizing)
- organize, sustain and participate in broad collective efforts (collaborative enquiry)
- create safe space for testing limits (serious playing).

We suggest that there are also some *hidden,* or ignored, themes relating to the sometimes messy realities of organizational life and the complex dynamics of human relationships and motivations. Most of the literature we reviewed is consensualist and rationalist and is based on hidden assumptions that all that is required to make succession planning work is for leaders to take their responsibilities seriously by writing and implementing a plan. This implicit view fails to take account of the importance of organizational culture and the potentially positive role of conflict in stimulating organizational growth (see Parker [2000] for a penetrating analysis of organizational culture which challenges the consensualist view and is relevant to all aspects of organizational life, including succession planning). Another unexamined view in the literature that we reviewed is that strategy making is entirely the responsibility of senior managers. A wider range of approaches is thus ignored (Fulop and Linstead, 1999). The potential impact on succession planning of specialist networks and inter-organizational relations is also not considered.

There are problems too with the stated assumptions. For example, why is succession planning elevated to a professional and ethical obligation? Why isn't it simply presented as a pragmatic requirement of a healthy professional and organizational body? In addition, workforce planning and succession planning are conflated in this body of literature to the extent that distinctions between them are not clearly made. This is important from our point of view because workforce planning, even for the cancer and palliative care workforce, is not our specific area of interest here, even though we recognize its importance. Indeed, workforce planning is of central importance in that specialists must inevitably be drawn from a pool of individuals in the general professional workforce.

Recent and current initiatives within our circle of concern

As stated earlier, Covey's (1999) idea of the 'circle of concern' is our starting point for thinking about succession planning in the specialist workforce in cancer and palliative care. Covey argues that a circle of concern is often so wide that it is not at first easy to see how one may make any impact on it (*Figure 5.2a*). He suggests that confining your attention to acting within a narrower range that is your sphere of influence will, over time, have the effect of reducing the dimension of the circle of concern as the scope of the 'sphere of influence' increases (*Figures 5.2b* and *5.2c*). The effect is to maximize ability to address selected elements of the circle of concern. There is a circle of concern in modern healthcare services which focuses on continuing to raise and maintain the levels of knowledge and skill in the whole cancer and palliative care workforce; however, our circle of concern in this book and in this chapter focuses mostly on specialist practice. The following examples show how various stakeholders are working within their sphere of influence to have an impact on that circle of concern.

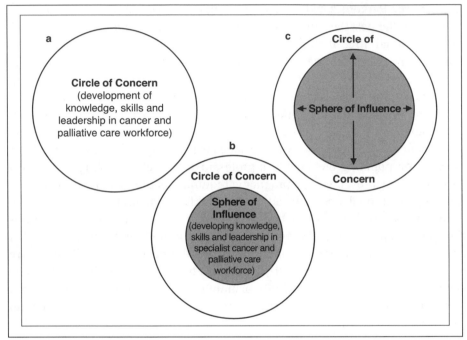

Figure 5.2: Circle of concern (a), circle of concern and initial sphere of influence (b) and circle of concern and expanding sphere of influence (c) (after Covey, 1999)

Developing generalists

There have been a number of development schemes in recent years which it is hoped will have an impact on succession planning in the broader sense of growing a new set of professionals (Woodhouse, 2002) and ensuring the availability of leaders for the future (Tahan, 2002) in cancer and palliative care.

Specialist cancer and palliative care nurses have developed link-practitioner schemes with nurses and AHPs in clinical areas who have an interest in the specialty, want to develop their knowledge and skills and aim to be a resource for their colleagues. These schemes are often difficult to establish, maintain and evaluate, but where they do appear to be successful one effect can be to stimulate and develop staff in readiness for recruitment to a specialist role. Success in these link-practitioner schemes is underpinned by a strong educational infrastructure in which participants have the opportunity to attend regular, structured educational sessions and may also undertake formal qualifications in the specialty.

Many NHS trusts offer secondments into cancer and palliative care teams, either to cover planned absences of permanent staff or as specific development opportunities. Such secondments enable participants to acquire knowledge, skills and experience of working at a specialist level, which they can take back to their area of work at the end of the secondment to influence patient care. More significantly, from the point of view of succession planning, successful secondments prepare staff to apply for specialist posts in the future, either within the seconding organization or elsewhere. Neither of these two specific approaches to succession planning in the British healthcare system appeared in our review of the literature, although they are based on transferable principles and form part of the range of activities embedded in current practice.

Macmillan Cancer Relief's recent initiatives in the area of succession planning range across the continuum, from growing the next generation of professionals (many of the programmes described in other chapters of this book) to preparing specialists to move into leadership roles in management, teaching and research.

Developing specialists

Macmillan Management Fellowship

This programme enables experienced Macmillan postholders to gain experience of the work of a Macmillan regional service development team. Management fellows are seconded from their partner organizations for 2 days per week for 15 months. During this time they have a work-experience placement in a Macmillan service development team, with individual mentorship from one of the team. Participants also undertake a postgraduate certificate in management and leadership at the Nuffield Institute for Health at the University of Leeds. This scheme was piloted by the Macmillan National Institute of Education (MNIE) in 2002–2003. At the time of writing, five management fellows have completed the programme and most have subsequently taken on more advanced leadership roles in the NHS and in Macmillan Cancer Relief.

Macmillan Teaching Fellowship

This is a parallel programme offered within MNIE. Fellows are seconded from partner organizations on placement to designated Macmillan education units across the UK. The secondment period is 15 months, with individual mentorship from a Macmillan lecturer. During the fellowship, teaching fellows expand their knowledge and expertise in learning and teaching through work-based learning by contributing to MNIE and university programmes. They also undertake a postgraduate certificate in teaching and learning in higher education. Three cohorts have completed this programme and a number of participants have subsequently moved into educational or leadership posts.

Macmillan Research Fellowship and Scholarship

This programme is the third strand of this scheme; it is designed to boost research capacity. This programme funds experienced clinical or teaching staff to undertake part-time doctoral study in an aspect of clinical care. Two fellowships are offered biannually, with four fellowships currently under way. The scheme was expanded in 2005 to include support for post-doctoral work. A number of annual research scholarships, consisting of smaller amounts of funding to support research training, are also available.

Leadership development

Leadership development programme

Leadership skills were identified as a development need for Macmillan postholders through educational profiling. A pilot Leadership Development programme, commissioned from the Centre for Development of Health Policy and Practice at the University of Leeds, was delivered in 2004 to two cohorts of Macmillan postholders. Each group consisted of 10 participants, one comprising clinical nurse specialists (CNSs) and the other a mixture of CNSs and AHPs. The programme was based on a 360° assessment instrument – the Leadership Effectiveness AnalysisTM.

These programmes were well received by participants. *"A very stimulating, challenging and motivating programme"* was a typical comment reported in the immediate post-course evaluation. In telephone interviews 6 months later, participants reported a number of positive changes in their leadership behaviour, including being more strategic, decisive, proactive, structured and consensual. Importantly, participants identified the process of change initiated by the programmes as complex and not subject to a simple cause-and-effect mechanism.

It became clear from these programmes that the process of undertaking a 360o assessment of leadership behaviour, with skilled feedback, was helpful in developing both understanding and skills. It also appeared that such skills-based leadership programmes, appropriate to the needs of specialist practitioners in cancer and palliative care, were not widely available. After wide-ranging discussion, and research into the variety and costs of the 360o instruments available, MNIE created a 12-month programme comprising completion of the NHS Leadership Qualities Framework (LQF) followed by a series of bimonthly action learning sets. At the time of writing, approximately 60 Macmillan postholders from a wide range of disciplines have registered for this programme and are in the process of completing the LQF.

All these initiatives reflect the key themes and processes identified in the conceptual framework previously presented. They demonstrate that trusts, teams of professionals and voluntary agencies can work in partnership to display a sense of professional, ethical and pragmatic duty to prepare and support the continuing development of the specialist workforce in cancer and palliative care against a background, for some, of many competing priorities. Appraisal, support for professional development and planning (key processes in our conceptual framework) may be varied in relation to some of the schemes outlined, but it is evident that these three sets of activities are important underpinnings of the initiatives.

Learning relationships (our key theme) are central to the success of each of these schemes. A high degree of motivation is required for individuals to pursue these development activities. There is often an element of risk-taking on their part in submitting themselves to an arduous path in which their commitment and performance may be under scrutiny. At the same time, there is a contract which obliges organizations to offer support in the form of mentorship, supervision and role modelling. This contract is based not only on ethical and pragmatic principles, but also on learning principles that recognize ways in which adults learn effectively.

Conclusion

Clearly there is much ambiguity in how succession planning is defined and interpreted. At executive level, effective succession planning can deliver top performers ready for the challenges of the future. However, the purpose of succession planning is not solely to fill specific positions in the future, as gaps in leadership and leadership development are major issues in contemporary health care. Indeed, many individuals have their own objectives and vision and seek out those who might assist them with their developmental needs (Hope-Smeltzer, 2002).

Successful succession planning can also enhance organizational cohesiveness and help to ensure high-quality patient care in a climate of continuing change and in the context of a flexible and mobile workforce (Kaminsky, 1997). Succession planning needs to begin with line managers and continue across the organization (Fruth, 2003).

Succession planning is a management responsibility, but there is no simple template for effectiveness as each organization has different needs. Assessment and appraisal systems that can measure the development of knowledge, skills and competence within organizations are of central importance (Butler and Roche-Tarry, 2002).

There are many obstacles to systematic planning for succession. These include (Abrams, 2002):

- greater emphasis on day-to-day operational activity
- lack of vision
- inconsistency between strategy and vision
- failure to take the long-term view.

Common mistakes in succession planning include (Tyler, 2002):

- being perceived as a single event rather than a process
- failure to anticipate the concerns of key personnel
- underestimating the planning time involved.

Succession planning needs to be understood as an investment that leads to the creation of defined career pathways and improved recruitment and retention. The appraisal process could be a powerful tool to identify the hidden talent at all levels in organizations and could be utilized to foster a high performance culture that is better adapted to survival in a rapidly changing environment (McConnell, 1996).

References

Abrams MN (2002) Succeeding at succession planning. *Health Forum J* **45**(1): 27–9

Bower FL (2000) Succession planning: a strategy for taking charge. *Nurs Leadersh Forum* **4**(4): 110–15

Butler K, Roche-Tarry DE (2002) Drawing a blueprint for succession. *Provider* **28**(11): 51–3

Byham WD, Nelson GD (1999) Succession planning: developing the next generation of leaders. *Health Forum J* **42**(6): 19, 24–6

Corso JA (2002) Measuring leadership: measuring what counts for succession planning. *Semin Nurse Manag* **10**(4): 265–8

Covey S (1999) *The Seven Habits of Highly Effective People*. Simon & Schuster UK Ltd, London

Fruth R (2003) Begin succession planning today. *Nurs Manage* **34**(9): 12

Fulop L, Linstead S (1999) *Management: A critical text*. Macmillan Press, London

Hope-Smeltzer C (2002) Succession planning. *J Nurs Adm* **32**(12): 615

Kaminsky RM (1997) Succession planning: a long-overlooked need. *Caring* **16**(4): 76–7

McConnell CR (1996) Succeeding with succession planning. *Health Care Superv* **15**(2): 69–78

Parker M (2000) *Organisational Culture and Identity: Unity and division at work*. Sage, London

Pulce R (2002) Optimizing human capital through succession planning. *Semin Nurse Manag* **10**(4): 225

Smith EL (2002) Leadership development: the heart of succession planning. *Semin Nurse Manag* **10**(4): 234–9

Soares DC (2002) Developing a succession plan: the North Bronx Healthcare Network. *Semin Nurse Manag* **10**(4): 228–33

Tahan HA (2002) Relationship management: a key strategy for effective succession planning. *Semin Nurse Manag* **10**(4): 254–64

Tyler JL (2002) Succession planning: charting a course for the future. *Trustee* **55**(6): 24–8

Woodhouse B (2002) Succession planning: lessons from the legal field. *Semin Nurse Manag* **10**(4): 269–73

CHAPTER 6

An overview of other MNIE initiatives

*Gail Johnston, Maxine Astley-Pepper, Fiona Whyte, Nici Evans,
Mary Mahoney, Eileen Mullard, Brian Nyatanga*

This chapter takes a different approach from other chapters in the book. It attempts to capture the importance and impact of other, shorter innovative Macmillan National Institute of Education (MNIE) programmes that were also influential in supporting Macmillan postholders throughout the UK. This chapter is therefore multi-authored, with each author focusing on a specific programme that he/she was leading in its development and delivery with the support of other MNIE lecturers.

The following programmes are reported on:

- The MNIE Conference
- 'Setting Out'
- Educational seminars
- Masterclass
- Managing breathlessness in patients with advanced cancer.

Unfortunately, we are unable to report on the lymphoedema programme as this was not ready at the time of submission of the manuscript for publication.

The MNIE Conference
Gail Johnston

The MNIE Conference 'Real Practice, Real Evidence' was established following a need, defined by profiling, to provide Macmillan postholders who had little or no experience in conference presenting with the opportunity to 'showcase' their work at a national forum attended by their peers. The conference was held annually in a major city in each of the four nations, including Birmingham, Cardiff, Edinburgh and Belfast, from 2001 to 2004.

Postholders from any discipline were invited to submit an abstract of their work under four main themes for oral or poster presentation. The themes were: research and evaluation; quality and audit; user involvement; and initiatives in service development. Help and support in writing abstracts was offered to postholders across the UK through the Macmillan education units.

A multidisciplinary panel with representatives from each region graded the abstracts for clarity, relevance to cancer and palliative care, interest to delegates, originality, completeness and potential for being a worthwhile presentation. The authors of the 16 highest scoring abstracts were then invited to present orally. The others were offered the opportunity to present posters if they had met a suitable standard.

The format of the conference was the same each year, with four themed sessions running twice, once in the morning and once in the afternoon. This allowed delegates to attend two of the four sessions throughout the day. Between sessions, delegates could view the posters or visit stands held by the Macmillan Professional Resources programme, the Macmillan research units or the pharmaceutical sponsors. Each themed session was chaired by a representative with a particular interest or reputation in the specific concurrent theme from a different part of the UK, and each of these chairpersons gave a small keynote speech before or after the session.

Around 800 postholders from different regions and disciplines, including nurses, doctors, allied health professionals (AHPs) and information officers attended the conferences over the 4-year period. Qualitative comments from the conference evaluations showed that postholders benefited from the chance to network with colleagues, share new initiatives in cancer and palliative care and develop confidence in their presentation skills in a safe environment among their peers.

When asked about the most valuable aspect of the conference in Belfast, delegates' responses included:

"Greater depth of knowledge about Macmillan and range of activities taking place UK wide in cancer services."

"Increased awareness of others' roles/opportunity to describe own role/multidisciplinary working."

"Encouragement/inspiration to present own work in future."

"Confidence/achievement in presenting own work."

From the MNIE perspective, the conference provided a platform for many specialist practitioners who probably would not have had the confidence to submit an abstract, let alone present to such a big audience. Through MNIE, support was offered in abstract writing, poster development and presentation skills, and as a result many specialist practitioners have now gone on to present or publish their work to a wider audience.

Unfortunately, we could not continue offering these conferences owing to funding restrictions, but we hope that the 4 years over which they were held proved beneficial to all who took part.

'Setting Out'
Maxine Astley-Pepper

'Setting out' is a unique programme developed to facilitate the role transition from generalist to specialist practitioner for Macmillan postholders working in palliative care. This innovative, dynamic 3-day course, delivered over 6 months, was devised in 1999 as a direct response to postholders' need for support during their role transition. Despite changes in education and the introduction of government legislation, eg. *Agenda for Change* (Department of Health [DH], 2001), the programme continues to be relevant today. Working with Macmillan service development managers, postholders are recruited to the programme within the first 12 months of their first, substantive Macmillan specialist practitioner role.

The programme content aims to raise awareness of workforce issues. At the outset the basis for the programme content was very much directed and influenced by the needs of each group; however, it soon became apparent that certain themes and issues were common to all groups, and evaluation and collation enabled a generic programme to be developed. A recent evaluation review indicates that the listed aims remain unchanged. These are:

* role transition
* team-working
* self and learning
* operational issues
* context of the role
* management – time, self and clinical decision-making.

The format for the first 2 days includes:

* mapping of the postholder's experience to date
* discussion about the process of role transition from generalist to specialist practitioner. This also includes the psychology of transition (discussed in depth in *Chapter 4*)

- workshops and exercises, eg. team dynamics
- presentations from other disciplines, eg. information managers, modern matrons, therapy teams
- reflective practice, focusing on experiences, clinical decision-making and self-awareness
- overview of current political trends and influences and the impact upon service provision and delivery
- service-side presentations, aligning operational issues to Macmillan's agenda and the political climate
- exploration of the components of the specialist practitioner role
- setting of individual objectives for the next 6 months, to be reviewed on day 3
- opportunity to book a Macmillan educational profile
- evaluation of the 2-day programme.

Day 3 takes place 6 months after day 2. Attendance varies; however, those attending value the opportunity to reflect on their progress and discuss new ways of working. The format is as follows:

- objectives are discussed and problem-solving within the group is invited
- the whole programme is evaluated.

At the end of the programme, the postholders will be able to:

- recognize, understand and discuss the components of the specialist role
- plan and assess their individual methods of workload management
- implement and adapt methods/strategies for effective time management
- recognize the limitations and challenges of working at specialist level
- further explore the complexity of team dynamics, and the issues that may arise, through discussion and self-exploration
- apply the process of role transition to their own circumstances, identifying where they may be on the 'transition curve'
- identify how change management may impact on their role, and discuss how they may respond appropriately.

History

'Setting Out' was developed by a MNIE working group of six Macmillan lecturers looking to revise the 'Introduction to Your Role' programme.

'Setting Out' was initially intended for clinical nurse specialists – as this was the largest Macmillan postholder group – to enable them to comply with the descriptors for specialist practice (United Kingdom Central Council for Nursing, Midwifery and Health Visiting [UKCC], 1995). The popularity and success of 'Setting Out' and the expanding diversity of the workforce means that the programme is now tailored to include all Macmillan AHPs.

The popularity of 'Setting Out' seems to be due to its format of self-direction, peer group support, relevant themes and topics and the opportunity to raise work-related issues in a safe forum outside the workplace.

Finlayson *et al* (2002) discuss the general decline in nursing figures in the UK; causes include burnout, stress and work-life imbalance. This invariably has an impact on patients and their families. In order to retain valuable cancer and palliative care postholders, MNIE, through 'Setting Out', endeavours to enable staff to undergo the (often traumatic) transitional phase of generalist to specialist practitioner. Support and nurturing are essential during this fragile stage in order to reduce emotional exhaustion or burnout (Cutcliffe *et al*, 2001).

Focus of the programme

'Setting Out' raises postholders' awareness of professional and socio-political influences that often impact on their practice, in addition to developing their expertise.

This innovative programme is responsive to need and allows for reflection and discussion in a supportive environment. Each programme is evaluated. A recent review shows that it is in line with government trends and policies, eg. *Agenda for Change* (DH, 2001) and *The NHS Knowledge and Skills Framework* (DH, 2004).

The programme is a catalyst for Macmillan postholders, enabling and encouraging them to access other Macmillan programmes, such as seminars themed around current issues, at which there is a great opportunity to share good practice and network on a national level. 'Setting Out' is a precursor to the individual educational review process known as Macmillan profiling (see *Chapter 2*). This involves a meeting between the individual postholder and a Macmillan lecturer from his/her local Macmillan education unit. The framework of the meeting is set around identifying past clinical and educational experience, the nature of the postholder's present post and the educational needs that have to be met in order for the postholder to fulfil that role.

The ultimate goal of 'Setting Out' is to improve patient care through improved professional practice.

Conclusion

To date, evaluation has clearly demonstrated that 'Setting Out' has fulfilled its aim to support Macmillan postholders in achieving a successful role transition to specialist practice. The programme offers the first real platform for postholders who are new in the role to network and understand their own role boundaries and the components of specialist practice. In addition, 'Setting Out' aims to foster the realities of independent practice, which include managing themselves, their time and prioritizing work demands. Some practitioners will be expected to work effectively with multidisciplinary team colleagues for the first time, and this programme takes a confidence-building approach, creating an environment for sharing ideas and problems. Finally, the programme has been successful in encouraging postholders to identify and implement previously acquired skills (transferable skills) in their new specialist role. This ability is the key to moving forward quickly in any new specialist role.

MNIE believes that this model can be used with other practitioners making a similar role transition.

References

Cutcliffe JR, Butterworth T, Proctor B (2001) *Fundamental Themes in Clinical Supervision.* Routledge, London

Department of Health (2001) *Agenda for Change: Modernising the NHS pay system.* DH, London

Department of Health (2004) *The NHS Knowledge and Skills Framework (NHS KSF) and Development Review Process.* DH, London

Finlayson B, Dixon J, Meadows S, Blair G (2002) Mind the gap: the extent of the NHS nursing shortage. *BMJ* **325**(7363): 538–44

UKCC (1995) *PREP and You.* UKCC, London

Educational seminars

Fiona Whyte, Nici Evans and Mary Mahoney

Historically, Macmillan Cancer Relief provided annual education seminars for their staff, which were usually delivered by external presenters. The seminars were held in a few selected locations in England and every postholder on the database was invited to attend free of charge. After the establishment of MNIE in 1998, these seminars became the responsibility of the lecturers working within MNIE. Subsequently the events were further developed and redesigned in response to direct need. These needs were identified through educational profiling of postholders throughout the four nations of the UK. A summary of needs identified via profiling was categorized annually and a programme of seminars was designed to respond to the most frequently identified needs.

Before the establishment of MNIE there was a perception that some Macmillan postholders frequently attended the seminars, while others never attended them. In early 1999, a structured questionnaire was designed internally by MNIE and sent to all postholders on the Macmillan postholder database, enquiring about the perceived value of the seminars. The postholders were also asked questions relating to why they attended or did not attend seminars. A response rate of more than 60% was achieved and a report was subsequently written and submitted to the charity's chief executive.

The respondents universally valued the educational component of the seminars and declared that the content was the prime reason for attending or not attending. However, it became apparent that some postholders would never be able to attend the seminars at weekends. In response to this, a few seminars have been held midweek and Thursday to Saturday in all subsequent years. Some respondents also commented that although they would like to attend, they could not travel to the events as they were held too far from their base. In response to these comments, the events are now held annually in all four nations.

It is important to note that in the section 'Any other comments' in the evaluation, respondents commonly expressed their appreciation to Macmillan for providing the annual seminars, and frequently thanked Macmillan for 'valuing' them. This perception of being 'valued' as a result of being able to attend a seminar on an annual basis is a recurring theme in the evaluation forms returned with every seminar since their creation.

> *"I always feel valued as a Macmillan postholder, and this seminar makes me feel very valued, something my local health authority cannot do. Thank you Macmillan."*

"This was my first seminar and I must say the Macmillan facilitators have been absolutely excellent. I have felt supported personally and professionally. I have felt looked after, comfortable and, most importantly, valued. I would like to say thank you to all involved and especially the charity."

A seminar is commonly defined as:

'... a meeting of specialists who may have different skills but specific common interests, who come together for the purposes of education and or training.'

In MNIE we also believe that any educational seminar should ideally work from the premise of 'investment and return'; indeed, this ideal has underpinned the development of all our educational seminars. As a result, the seminars provide individuals with material that is of direct relevance and use to them in their daily work while, at the same time, delivering it in a manner that respects them personally as adult learners and in an environment that instils value in them. We believe that it can reasonably be presumed that a significant percentage of participants will use the seminar material and, in our case, use it ultimately to benefit patients and others affected by cancer. Once this educational strategy and ideal was adopted, it was relatively easy to develop seminar topics in response to identified need.

Delivery of seminars

The seminar event spans a 3-day period, starting at 6.00pm on the first evening, continuing through the next day and finishing with lunch on the final day. Most seminars take place over a weekend. This means they start at 6.00pm on Friday night (usually), finishing with dinner at 8.00pm, and utilize all day Saturday (9.00am to 4.30pm) and Sunday morning (9.00am until 12.30pm) as seminar time.

The events are provided free of charge to participants, and are held throughout the UK; venues are either hotels with conference facilities or specific conference/training centres. The venues have all been chosen carefully in the belief that, as participants are fully committed to coming to these events in their own time, using up their precious weekends to attend, it would be even more conducive to learning if the events were held in comfortable venues with a reputation for high standards of accommodation and food. The seminars involve considerable administration, and their success would not be possible without the continuous expert support and administration from the conference team within Macmillan Cancer Relief and the MNIE administrators.

The first evening of the seminar programme frequently comes at the end of a busy working day or week for the delegates. The fact that the work of a Macmillan postholder is frequently stressful and emotionally draining is taken into account, and the first evening is designed to introduce the topic for the seminar in a lightweight, and where possible, fun way. This format creates an awareness of the seminar material to come and encourages participants to get to know each other and relax before gathering for dinner. It is one of the jobs of the seminar facilitators to ensure that everyone is made welcome; this is especially important for postholders who have attended on their own or for the first time. The problem of a postholder attending as a single delegate was highlighted in the original questionnaire. Two such individuals commented that no-one had spoken to them for the whole weekend and so they did not intend to attend a seminar again.

The main material is presented at the Saturday session. Because all MNIE staff are professionally qualified teachers, the material is underpinned with formal learning aims and outcomes. Participants have subscribed to these before attending the programme. In order to facilitate adult learning, this day-long session is broken down into one semi-formal signposting session followed by small group workshops.

The final morning begins with facilitated networking, where issues of interest, topics or projects suggested by the delegates on the first evening form the basis of discussion forums. Over the weekend, each delegate signs up for a session of interest to him/her. The sessions are run by the delegates themselves, with the seminar facilitators on standby to provide help or advice if necessary. The inclusion of specific formal networking time came about, once again, in response to an identified need. Historically, Macmillan breast care nurses had their own annual seminar, but as the numbers and varieties of postholders grew it became obvious that providing site-specific or role-specific seminars had become impossible. This networking time thus allows like-minded people to get together and has proven very successful.

> *"Networking was very helpful and allowed me to discuss my anxieties with like-minded people – problems solved!"*

It has been noted that this formal networking often promotes long-term contact and mutual support between like-minded postholders in many different parts of the UK. Some entire teams of staff choose to attend the same seminar, which has the added value of promoting team bonding both during and after the formal sessions; some of the teams also choose to work together on the third morning to develop team projects.

The 3-day event ends with a final hour-long semi-formal session. This session will aim to provide either another complementary point of view on the subject under consideration or a focus to draw together the salient lessons and learning from the seminar. Interestingly, the delegates, who in the main are going back to work on the following day, frequently report going back to work feeling refreshed and with renewed enthusiasm and vigour.

"I have been a postholder for 14 years and always look forward to these seminars as I always go back to work re-energized and refreshed and ready to put into practice what I have learnt. This seminar is no different. Thank you Macmillan."

At the end of the seminar, every attendee is encouraged to fill out an open evaluation form, which takes the form of one A4 sheet of paper with the solitary question 'How valuable has the event been for you?' printed at the top of the page. This open question has, in the main, generated a very detailed response, and every form is sent to head office for their consideration, along with a general seminar evaluation summary. This open and transparent evaluation has ensured that Macmillan Cancer Relief is aware of the programme's success and has facilitated the refining of programmes where necessary.

As the professional Macmillan workforce grows and moves slowly away from the nurse as the most common postholder, to the inclusion of more doctors and all types of AHP, social workers and care coordinators on the database, the seminars have been developed to be useful to all postholders, and issues and topics covered are always relevant to all groups.

"This seminar was very practically based and met all my expectations/ needs as an occupational therapist. It was not nurse specific or any other profession orientated, which was really good."

"The seminar content bridged all disciplines and was not just nurse specific, which was exciting and valuable. I felt like part of the Macmillan family."

In the past, the medical postholders and Macmillan-badged teachers and researchers had their own educational seminars, although doctors can and do attend the general seminars. Specific seminars have also been provided for AHPs and social workers, although the evaluations of these indicated that most postholders preferred multiprofessional seminars; indeed, it is felt that the more multiprofessional the seminar, the greater the understanding of other professional roles that can be fostered and the greater the multidisciplinary working that can be encouraged. A final group of postholders who have been provided with their own seminar in recent years are postholders in specific lead roles; these seminars have been entitled Masterclasses and are considered in this chapter by Eileen Mullard and Brian Nyatanga.

Originally, MNIE provided two educational seminar topics every year, but this proved to be very costly in development time; also, it was clear from the seminar evaluation forms that postholders would have liked to attend both programmes. So, with this in mind, the programme was redesigned as two seminar programmes delivered over a 2-year period; this meant that participants could come to programme A in year one and programme B in year two. This has proved very successful both for seminar participants and for developers.

The seminars are facilitated by MNIE lecturers in partnership with Macmillan service development managers. This dual facilitation has provided an excellent integrated model for ensuring that postholders are supported by management and education. The service development managers make themselves available throughout the weekend for discussion of relevant service and managerial issues and offer work-related support. This has been offered in a semi-formal way via a service development manager surgery during the networking slot on the third morning, but it is important to note that this support and advice continues informally during all breaks and meals throughout the 3-day period.

"The presence of the service development manager for both discussion and advice was invaluable and very encouraging."

Seminar topics

Recent seminar topics (and their titles) include:

- quality and audit ('It's not what you do, it's the way that you do it')
- communication issues ('So you think you are a good communicator!')
- coping with change ('Surviving in a constantly changing environment')
- teaching skills ('Tips and tools for teaching in everyday practice').

The titles are designed to reflect the informality of the seminars, whereby the aims and learning outcomes clearly state what can be expected from the educational input. The seminar that examined communication skills was funded by a partner charity, and part of the funding agreement allowed external professional researchers to examine whether the education in the seminar made any difference to clinical practice. The very strong valid and reliable findings suggested that the seminar was, indeed, making a clear and positive difference to the participants' communication skills with patients and others affected by cancer. These findings were very exciting for MNIE and a clear indication of one way in which education was directly influencing practice.

Conclusion

 In today's climate of health spending, cutbacks and health authority deficits, Macmillan Cancer Relief has run educational seminars that are accessible to all their professional postholders, in the belief that offering education over a 3-day period, in a comfortable venue, provides postholders with education and support to positively influence practice. A sense of charity ownership and pride has been created, which instils value in postholders.

The belief and conviction of MNIE is that by investing in those who will ultimately care for people affected by cancer, those affected by cancer can expect a return in the form of evidence-based practice and best possible care, from a well-educated and supported workforce. In 2005, these seminars were attended by 865 postholders from all four countries in the UK, thereby promoting the same care and service in all four nations. We believe that the expense of these events, when considered under the umbrella of investment return, is money well spent, and that the ultimate beneficiaries are the people affected by cancer. What all the participants and MNIE jointly aim to do through these seminars is to make a difference to the experience of all those affected by cancer.

Masterclass programme
Eileen Mullard and Brian Nyatanga

This programme was developed in 2000 in response to the emergence of lead nurses and the increased expectation on them to understand and implement strategic plans while influencing policy in health care. This was also a time when the role of the Macmillan specialist was further evolving. This change occurred in response to implementation of the *The NHS Cancer Plan* (DH,

2000), *The Gold Standards Framework for Palliative Care* (DH, 2003a) and other NHS new directives. The impact of these changes was highlighted through profiling, as discussed in *Chapter 2*, and in feedback from seminars, as reported by Fiona Whyte and colleagues above. MNIE deemed it important to acknowledge that the demands placed upon lead practitioners were no longer being addressed adequately through the seminars offered to specialist practitioners. It was this realization that led to the development of the Masterclass programme, with a specific focus on how to function and lead effectively in a strategic and political healthcare environment.

Aim of the programme

The aim of the Masterclass programme is to offer newly created lead cancer and palliative care practitioners and nurse consultants support in their roles in the face of constantly changing demands in cancer and palliative care.

The role of lead practitioners

The lead nurse practitioner roles were challenging in that, from their inception, lead nurse practitioners were expected to:

- work strategically, politically and influence policy agenda at boardroom level
- support and direct activities of the more junior specialists working with them
- implement government directives and, in some cases, ensure that targets were being met
- respond to the economic climate within health care, and in some cases manage small budgets.

At the same time as lead practitioners were facing numerous changes in the healthcare agenda, they were also going through their own role transition, which made it very difficult for most of them to be effective in these new roles.

In response, MNIE, which was created in 1998 by Macmillan Cancer Relief in partnership with seven host universities UK wide, developed a short and sharp Masterclass learning programme specifically for Macmillan lead practitioners. The Masterclass was seen as a rapid response to address the sudden demands and issues confronting the lead practitioners. The content was put together by MNIE lecturers with input from several lead practitioner representatives from the four nations (England, Wales, Northern Ireland and Scotland). The content reflected the pressing needs at the time and the whole ethos behind Masterclass was the element of flexibility, which enabled the programme to address new challenges coming from the Department of Health.

The topics covered included:

- working and thinking strategically
- working with and influencing politicians
- workforce planning and facilitating work-based learning
- understanding trends in cancer and palliative care (to include cancer statistics, epidemiology and economic evaluation)
- strategic planning (to include business and operational plans)
- how to implement government initiatives and directives, eg. National Service Frameworks (NSFs), *The NHS Cancer Plan* (DH, 2000), *Essence of Care* (NHS Modernisation Agency, 2006); *Improving Supportive and Palliative Care for Adults with Cancer* (National Institute for Clinical Excellence [NICE], 2004), *The Gold Standards Framework for Palliative Care* (DH, 2003a) and now *Agenda for Change* (DH, 2003b)
- latterly, the need to understand international influences, such as those from Europe and America, on UK healthcare systems.

Other topics were aimed at building confidence in the lead practitioners and included:

- understanding yourself, using the Myers–Briggs Type Indicator (Myers *et al*, 1998)
- developing your leadership skills using ideas from Kouzes and Posner (1997)
- presenting yourself (board level and image wise)
- negotiating and influencing skills.

Delivery of the Masterclass

At inception, the Masterclass programme was delivered twice a year over 2 days, from 5.00 pm the first day to 5.00 pm the following day, at different locations throughout the UK. Following an evaluation, a few changes were made to suit the participants. One key change was an alteration in the starting and finishing times: programmes were changed to run from 12.00 noon the first day to 12.00 midday the following day. The frequency of Masterclass programmes was also increased to four a year in response to increasing demand from the lead practitioners. Macmillan Cancer Relief funded the cost of this programme, and as this included accommodation there was no monetary cost to employers of the lead practitioners. The Masterclass programme was facilitated by MNIE lecturers and invited speakers who were experts in each of the topics on the programme. The programme also offered an opportunity for networking on the evening of the first day; this platform has been valued by all as it offers participants an opportunity to share experiences and help each other to solve problems occurring in the workplace. This networking idea has continued after the programme, with lead practitioners keeping in touch with each other.

Evaluation of the Masterclass programme

Evaluation offers a basis for improving the quality of any programme delivered, and it was important that such a process was also applied to Masterclass. At the end of each Masterclass (on day two) participants completed an evaluation form, commenting on the content and its relevance to their work. All the evaluations were treated seriously and fed back to MNIE, where changes and improvements were then agreed. The MNIE lecturers facilitating at each Masterclass also evaluated the programme from their perspective, which included level and pace of delivery, opportunities for interaction and group participation in discussions and overall conduciveness of the learning environment. It is important that the learning outcomes for the Masterclass programme are achieved by the end of day two, and the lecturers' evaluations tended to focus on this.

> *"Throughout the evaluations, the participants verbalized the invaluable mechanism for networking with like-minded professionals in strategic posts. This networking was highly valued and appreciated in a NHS climate that does not allow for this."*

Further comments from lead practitioners included:

> *"...feel valued by Macmillan and now re-charged to go back to my service and networks with fresh new ideas of 'living into a new possibility' and realizing the power of influence within myself."*
>
> *"I always think that if you take one or two thoughts or ideas away*

from an event such as this, then you are doing well. I have three: (1) to adopt a solutions-focused approach; (2) to allow everyone to be a contribution to health the service provision; (3) to flap my wings at least once a week!"

"This was beneficial for me at this crucial time for the service, as I was feeling mentally depleted, and yet now I am leaving with renewed energy and new strategies to apply to the service. The benefit will be felt across the service down to the patients."

"Felt empowered and energized with new ideas."

"I was impressed with how our facilitators helped us recognize our personal effectiveness in our roles and how to use positive ways of looking at mistakes."

Summary

The MNIE lecturers who developed the Masterclass programme valued the notion of 'user involvement' and therefore invited representatives from lead practitioners to input on the planning of topics to be covered over the year. By doing this, they are able to ensure that the Masterclass programmes respond closely to the immediate needs or challenges in cancer and palliative care and help lead practitioners to lead effectively.

We believe that this Masterclass programme was innovative and unique in the way that it responded to the sudden emergence of the nurse consultant role and lead practitioners. The programme's flexibility means that it can address the challenges, needs and demands encountered by lead practitioners and nurse consultants across the UK. The fact that the programme is developed and facilitated by MNIE lecturers guarantees high quality of the learning experience and relevance to practice. The funding of the provision of this programme in full by Macmillan Cancer Relief removes any financial constraints from the employer, allowing lead practitioners to attend and increase their repertoire of skills and knowledge.

The success of this programme is attributed to the vision of MNIE and financial support of Macmillan Cancer Relief and the host universities that have supported the lead practitioners to function more effectively in their new roles.

References

Department of Health (2000) *The NHS Cancer Plan: A plan for investment, a plan for reform*. DH, London

Department of Health (2003a) *The Gold Standards Framework: A programme for community palliative care*. DH, London

Department of Health (2003b) *Agenda for Change*. DH, London

Kouzes JM, Posner BZ (1997) *Leadership Practice Inventory*. Jossey-Bass, San Francisco, California

Myers IB, McCaulley MH, Quenk NL, Hammer AL (1998) *MBTI Manual (A guide to the development and use of the Myers-Briggs Type Indicator)*. 3rd edn. Consulting Psychologists Press, Palo Alto, California

National Institute for Clinical Excellence (2004) *Improving Supportive and Palliative Care for Adults with Cancer*. NICE, London

NHS Modernisation Agency (2006) *Essence of Care: Promoting health*. DH, London

Managing Breathlessness in Patients with Advanced Cancer
Elizabeth Wright and Claire Taylor

Background to the programme

Breathlessness is a common symptom in patients with advanced cancer and can lead to a much-reduced quality of life. Treatment for this has previously focused on pharmacological interventions, such as the use of opioids, and procedures such as drainage of pleural effusions (Corner *et al*, 1996).

The programme 'Managing Breathlessness in Patients with Advanced Cancer' was developed from research into the nursing management of breathlessness in patients with lung cancer using a range of therapeutic strategies (Bredin *et al*, 1999; Corner *et al*, 1996). The aim of the research was to ascertain whether a nursing approach to the management of breathlessness could be developed and evaluated using non-pharmacological approaches (Corner *et al*, 1996). The research, which involved two randomized control trials, demonstrated that this approach did make a difference to patients who were breathless.

Aims of the programme

The programme endorses this innovative approach to managing breathlessness and incorporates a range of strategies that can complement medical treatment for breathlessness. The programme was developed by researchers, educators and practitioners who had experience in the management of breathlessness. Central to the programme is the therapeutic relationship between the practitioner and his/her family and carers.

The aims of the programme are:

- to prepare health professionals with the skills necessary to undertake an accurate assessment of the person who is breathless due to advanced disease
- to provide health professionals with an opportunity to learn a range of skills that they can then use within the clinical setting to teach a person who is living with breathlessness how to cope with it
- to explore the psychological and social aspects of breathlessness for each individual
- to provide a peer group and safe environment in which to discuss the complexities of communicating and giving of self in practice
- to explore service planning and provision in the light of current political, social and practical contexts.

Delivery and content

The programme is aimed at health professionals – clinical nurse specialists, occupational therapists and physiotherapists – who have held a specialist post in cancer or palliative care. The programme is delivered over 8 days and includes three action learning groups. Skills-based, experiential workshops are used to develop advanced skills that underpin clinical practice, and to consider the theory and research in which the approach is rooted. These workshops include patient assessment, relaxation techniques, pacing, coping strategies and breathing retraining.

Evaluation

The programme has been well evaluated. A longitudinal evaluation has been undertaken to explore the impact of the pilot course on the participant's practice (Froggatt and Walford, 2005). This evaluation demonstrated that the course had a positive impact on participants' personal development and confidence in using the interventions when working with breathless patients. Course participants were also more prepared to engage with patients suffering from breathlessness, and therapeutic working was undertaken with patients from pre-diagnosis through to the terminal stages of illness.

A recent course participant commented that she was:

'... delighted to have had time to develop my therapeutic work with breathless patients. I am now able to approach this very distressing experience for patients in a more positive and enabling way. I think we have all come away with new knowledge that we can share with others'.

Conclusion

Attendance on this programme increases participants' confidence and competence in the management of breathless patients. This has the potential to impact positively on care for this group of patients. Furthermore, the framework of the programme, although linked to the management of breathlessness, develops skills that are directly transferable to other situations in the clinical setting.

References

Bredin M, Corner J, Krishnasamy M, Plan H, Bailey C, A'Hern R (1999) Multicentred randomized controlled trial of nursing intervention for breathlessness in patients with advanced cancer. *BMJ* **318:** 901–4

Corner J, Plant H, A'Hern R, Bailey C (1996) Non-pharmacological intervention for breathlessness in lung cancer. *Palliat Med* **10**(4): 299–305

Froggatt K, Walford C (2005) Developing advanced clinical skills in the management of breathlessness: an evaluation of an educational intervention. *Eur J Oncol Nurs* **9**(3): 269–79

Summary

This chapter has outlined some of the short but innovative programmes developed through MNIE to address the immediate needs of Macmillan practitioners identified through profiling. It is important here to acknowledge the time commitment and intensive effort required from all the lecturers for the development of such needs-responsive programmes. That vision and courage are needed to develop such programmes at short notice is undisputed, and this was only possible through the funding provided by Macmillan Cancer Relief. It is hoped that all the Macmillan postholders who attended these programmes found them beneficial to their own growth and development. The development of such programmes requires a strong team approach to working from all the lecturers, and this was clearly demonstrated in each of these programmes.

CHAPTER 7

Future directions in developing the workforce

Liz Searle, Suzanne Henwood

This final chapter outlines future challenges facing those engaged in developing the workforce. These challenges are viewed in the light of changing healthcare policy, workforce demands and the changing needs of people requiring care. The chapter concludes by offering a new, dynamic model for continuing professional development (CPD), which we consider to be appropriate for this changing environment.

The challenges ahead

Healthcare education faces many challenges in the future. This book has outlined one successful approach to meeting these challenges, namely a work-based learning model, which was used by Macmillan Cancer Relief to develop the cancer and palliative care workforce. This model was shown to be a robust and sustainable way of ensuring expert, competent practice while keeping the theory–practice gap as narrow as possible. The innovative, nationwide structure comprised multiple education units, which combined to form a virtual institute of education. This brought together six universities, with the formation of truly collaborative partnerships for developing new programmes and ways of working, as well as disseminating best practice, not only within those education units, but also across the wider education community. There can be no question of its success.

Macmillan postholders gained enormously from the Macmillan National Institute of Education (MNIE), which offered excellent educational and development support, helping to make them leaders in their field. However, the healthcare environment is constantly changing and the needs of patients are constantly being reviewed. In light of this, it is appropriate to ask how those professionals can best be supported in the future.

One thing is certain: high-quality training and development of staff is going to become even more vital in the future to enable health professionals to keep ahead of the changes, and senior staff to lead those changes, thereby ensuring that people requiring palliative care services receive first-class care – a position the Government would also welcome.

Since 1998 the NHS has increased its emphasis on personal and professional development. All NHS staff should by now have undergone an appraisal and have a development plan (although the evidence suggests that this is still not in place for all staff). Within the *Agenda for Change* (Department of Health [DH], 2004a) remit, all staff should also look at the knowledge and skills required to undertake their job and should build their development around filling any gaps. In addition, clinical governance promotes a joint responsibility for professional development around both the individual and the employer to ensure that all staff undertake effective CPD. The question for educators is 'What role should we play in the future?'

A unique aspect outlined in this book is planning development for practitioners. One advantage of involving educators in this role (beyond having the time to discuss development needs in depth on a one-to-one basis) is their ability to identify training needs for individuals, teams, organizations and whole specialties to ensure that courses and development activities meet the specific needs identified by clinical practitioners. If educators are not playing an active part in the needs identification process, they will also struggle to identify clinical educational needs, and there is a risk that subsequent education programmes will be irrelevant and unattractive.

From experience, it is clear that professional development planning must be inclusive to be effective. Individuals have to play an active part in the process. They have to truly reflect on their own ability and future objectives. They have to be willing to truly explore and get to know themselves in order to move forwards in a positive way. The employer and line manager also have to be a fully integrated part of the process to ensure that at least a proportion of the development needs are related to the work environment. Personal development is important, but it is professional development (that which impacts on the individual in the workplace or directly on the service provided) that is required to improve the care given to patients.

In addition, by jointly agreeing the development needs and considering how any new skills will be used in practice, the student is likely to encounter less opposition to implementing change following any development opportunity. It is the authors' belief that the educator is ideally placed to identify the best way to meet the development needs of the individual. The education team can help with the identification of learning styles, thereby ensuring that the most appropriate activity is sought and the correct amount of support is obtained to achieve a successful outcome. The education team (as part of a national network) is aware of development opportunities nationally and locally – this is a huge advantage of national networks or institutes, which can cover the whole of the UK and not only increase awareness of provision but also share best practice geographically. The educator can support the individual during that development time and, finally, can build new development opportunities led by the needs identified across the practice area.

Educators will also have a role in the future in terms of accreditation and validation of activities. While there will always be a place for informal CPD activities designed to meet individual need, within *Agenda for Change* (DH, 2004a) there is an increasing need to offer accredited courses that can demonstrate a level of attainment for the individual, which will be linked to his/her career and pay progression. In order to achieve advanced or consultant level, individuals are going to have to show that they can study at master's level and possibly beyond. While this does not necessarily mean they have to obtain a masters degree they will have to show that they can study at the right level, and accredited courses will help them achieve this. The challenge for educators is to ensure that appropriate and relevant master's degrees, which contribute to advanced practice, are available.

Agenda for Change is likely to impact on the whole area of staff development (at least for NHS staff covered by the new policy). The job evaluation aims to:

> '... *fairly reward people by measuring their job-related skills, knowledge and responsibilities ... to help ensure staff receive equal pay for work of equal value.'*
> (DH, 2004a)

The annual development review meeting should ensure that all staff meet to discuss development and devise a development plan, and then discuss how that development will be implemented in practice. We would argue that educators need to be part of that process to get maximum return on the time invested in it.

> '*The NHS KSF [Knowledge and Skills Framework] and associated development review process is about the NHS investing in the ongoing development of all its staff in the future. This will help to ensure that staff are supported to be effective in their jobs and committed to developing and maintaining high quality services for the public ... In turn, individual members of staff are expected to make a commitment to develop and apply their knowledge and skills to meet the demands of their post and work flexibly in the interests of the public.'*
> (DH, 2004b)

There can be no argument that education has to be a part of future professional practice.

One limitation of *Agenda for Change* – other than that it does not cover all staff in palliative care – is that it offers only 'a broad generic framework' (DH, 2004b) and does not explore individual attributes and specific or softer competencies, which can impact so much on how well a job is done. This is another reason to have a broader educator involved in development planning, namely to ensure that holistic development opportunities are considered.

In the UK, both professionals and patients are part of a society that remains death denying and fearing, yet their expectations of health care within terminal illness continue to rise. Clarity on what constitutes a good death has been sought for some time (Fordham *et al*, 1998) to help build appropriate care models. The need to reflect on this issue underpins the launch of a new National Alliance, supported by many palliative care organizations, to begin to understand what needs to change to make death and dying culturally better understood across a culturally diverse population (National Death Alliance, 2005). Education and research have to be central to that work and must go hand in hand with practice development. This chapter explores some of the key issues facing palliative care education, in the hope of generating local and national discussion and reflection to influence the future education strategy, which will work to maximize the patient care experience in death and dying.

It is reasonable to question whether the work-based learning model presented in this book will be able to meet the future challenges in cancer and palliative care services. Only by exploring, understanding and evaluating the challenges ahead (and our previous educational experiences), and being clear how we, as educators, are going to respond to those challenges, can we begin to answer this. We do not claim to have all the answers, but the experience of setting up and running MNIE has generated a wealth of data, which can be used to help ensure that education of the future learns from its mistakes and builds on its successes. It is in the spirit of shared learning that we present our experience of MNIE to you to maximize the learning potential from it. The following sections outline the changing healthcare context and the challenges to which education must respond.

Broadening the palliative care agenda

Pressure to extend the knowledge and skills developed in cancer palliative care to people with a wide range of long-term conditions has recently gained great momentum. In terms of equity, there can be no argument that all people requiring palliative care interventions both deserve, and have a right to expect, the same opportunity; in the past, however, this equity has not been apparent. *The National Service Framework for Long-Term Conditions* (DH, 2005) clearly emphasizes these requirements to broaden the palliative care agenda, and this poses significant challenges to healthcare professionals and educators, which could drastically change the nature of future provision of both services and education.

Palliative care services currently struggle to meet existing needs and certainly are not always delivering care in the setting of patients' choice (Wanless, 2002). If palliative care is to be extended to all people living with long-term conditions, then this demand is going to be even greater (King's Fund, 2002). One service redesign solution is to provide more palliative care in people's homes (Woods, 2002). This would also seem to be in line with patients' preferences, 75% of whom (Davies and Higginson, 2004) would prefer to receive end-of-life care at home. Yet recent reports show that only 20% of deaths occur at home, with 57% occurring in hospital and 17% in hospices (Davies and Higginson, 2004). Achieving the goal of allowing patients to choose where they die seems a long way off. England currently has one of the highest death-in-hospital rates compared with the USA and parts of Europe (Davies and Higginson, 2004).

One challenge facing professionals, carers and educators is how to transfer existing styles and models of palliative care to different disease groups. Feedback from the Government's £12 million initiative to extend end-of-life care to a wider group indicates that this is going to be more challenging than first thought.

This issue of prognosis, and subsequently the appropriate initiation and intervention of end-of-life care, has also been identified by Murray *et al* (2003) (*Figures 7.1a and b*).

This model shows that the illness trajectory for long-term conditions, such as heart failure, is vastly different from that for cancer. Questions need to be asked as to which aspects of care are transferable and how other aspects can be adapted. Consideration will also have to be given to how this is going to be evaluated before significant decisions are made about which disease groups should be included.

In addition to different disease groups, the presence of different care settings also poses a challenge. The healthcare environment has undergone significant restructuring over recent years and the recent boundary changes between acute and primary care only serve to further intensify this situation. The recent changes to the NHS structure announced by Sir Nigel Crisp, Chief Executive of the NHS, in his letter *Commissioning a Patient-Led NHS* (28 July 2005, Gateway ref: 5312) constitute the biggest change to the service since its inception. The splitting of provider and commissioning roles

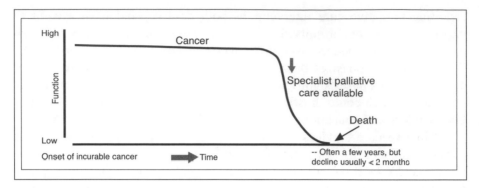

Figure 7.1a: Illness trajectory in cancer patients. (Reproduced from Murray et al (2003) BMJ 326(7385): 368, by kind permission of the author, Scott Murray, and the BMJ Publishing Group)

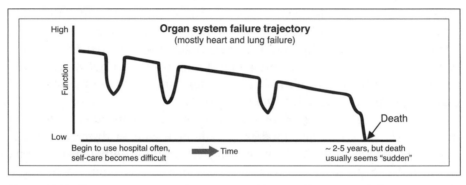

Figure 7.1b: Illness trajectory in long-term conditions. (Reproduced from Murray et al (2003) BMJ 326(7385): 368, by kind permission of the author, Scott Murray, and the BMJ Publishing Group)

and the intended removal of all provider services from primary care leaves many palliative care practitioners needing a new employment base. This single shift may inadvertently destroy the boundaries that have previously contributed to preventing people dying at home. We may now see many practitioners working across boundaries and the division between the acute sector and primary care may fade, but with this will come new learning requirements, which will need to be met.

Adequate development of practitioners who can adjust to these challenges will take more than just good initial educational preparation. Society will require practitioners who can push the boundaries, who can challenge policy and translate principles into new settings, who go on learning and generate a truly learning environment. Work-based learning as a model of development is well placed to prepare practitioners for this role, but issues around clinical leadership to complement the extended roles into specialist and consultant posts will need to be considered, alongside leadership coaching and clinical mentorship, which may not have been commonplace in the past.

Many of the historic strategic documents for health practitioners have explored what they might contribute to the future – *Making a Difference* (DH, 1999), *The NHS Plan* (DH, 2000) and *A Health Service of All the Talents* (DH, 2001). Many address the need to offer careers to practitioners that are both rewarding and flexible in their promotion opportunities. The subtext to this, of course, is the changing demographics and ever-depleting workforce, compounded by the move to increase primary care provision and offer more local services. The Royal College of Nursing (RCN) Labour Market Review 2002 (Buchan and Seccombe, 2003) shows that only one in eight of those on the register are under 30 today compared with one in four less than 10 years ago. Almost 100 000 registrants are aged 55 or older. The combination of changing structures and an ageing workforce is going to present significant challenges to service providers and educational providers in the future.

Specific workplace factors, including low staffing levels, may also have both a positive and a negative affect on those undertaking CPD. For example, a feeling of being overwhelmed at work is associated with a superficial and disorganized learning approach (Delva *et al*, 2002); conversely, physicians who believe that they have choice, independence and support in their work will take a deep approach to learning, are also internally motivated and will use independent learning methods (Delva *et al*, 2002).

If there are insufficient numbers of professionals to meet the future agenda, it is reasonable to ask who will be providing this widened palliative care service. Clearly, the development of programmes such as the 'Expert Patients Programme' (www.expertpatients.nhs.uk) is a move towards a new model of self-management, alongside the increased emphasis being placed on social care by organizations such as Macmillan Cancer Relief. Patients, carers, family and volunteers will all have a role to play in caring for the very sick and chronically ill patient at home.

Perhaps this social change will take death and dying back to the community where it belongs, and the aspirations of many to die at home can then once again be realistically considered. It is clear that a new focus on living more easily at home, increasing the amount and quality of information and the wider range of financial advice available are all geared to a new order of self-management, with less reliance on traditional healthcare professionals. Professionals who can navigate around the various options for care and services available will be required, to ensure that patients and carers are well supported in their new role.

The Department of Health has recently published a White Paper report on a public consultation – *Your Health, Your Care, Your Say* (DH, 2006). This may be the first time that the public have genuinely been asked their views on policy before it is written. This reflects a culmination of increasing public and user involvement. As this movement gains momentum, the discerning future customer – the patient – will begin to exert the right of a truly informed choice in his/her own care (Kendall, 2001), which may in time also overlap into ensuring appropriate educational provision for his/her carers.

It is therefore not inconceivable that future education programmes will have students drawn from this diverse group. There is a good chance that patients, patients' families, carers, volunteers and professionals will all be learning together for some subjects. Patients and carers will take on a new role as active learning partners, not just sharers of experiences. One can only hope that this partnership will be less fraught than previous experiences of professional multidisciplinary working, which generated significant challenges for those involved. As we move to a health service that sees the patient at its epicentre, it is reasonable to suggest that education should follow – a significant challenge for education providers of the future.

In considering how this might become a reality, the concept of work-based learning, which revolves around partnership learning, crosses several care contexts and genuinely involves patients and carers, again becomes a possibility. Indeed, it could be proposed that work-based learning, with active participation of all stakeholders, is the only education model that will meet the needs of both the changing education agenda and the workforce.

Educators for the future

As highlighted earlier, demographics show a reduction in the numbers of practitioners in clinical practice. This is true of both generalist and specialist staff. It also means a reduction in the number of educators who can be drawn from that field. Age alone is not the only issue impacting on this group. Currently, pay and terms and conditions for academics employed in universities have lost pace with the new pay deals for clinical staff in the NHS. The salary of ward managers now on Band 7 (*Agenda for Change*) exceeds that offered to lecturers. In addition, the policy focus on palliative care has led to a plethora of new roles: project leads, consultant nurses and allied health professionals (AHPs), lead nurses, extended scope practitioners, end-of-life initiatives coordinators and community matrons, to name a few. These offer an interesting and varied number of career paths for those remaining in clinical care.

In contrast, academics are under pressure to meet teaching contact hours, publish and be research active to meet the Research Assessment Exercise

– a move that has not been completely without cost. There is a real risk that teaching multiple hours of an emotional subject such as palliative care to ever-increasing class sizes will lead to increased stress and loss of job satisfaction, and that staff will be attracted back into the clinical environment where they can see career progression opportunities and improving pay and conditions.

In an attempt to reduce contact hours for staff and widen access to education for the reducing number of students, e-learning has found some new champions. The growth in e-learning for palliative care subjects does widen access to materials. However, as reducing death anxiety and enhancing standards requires students to explore their own mortality, distance learning may not be the most appropriate format and may result in high attrition rates as students struggle to study such difficult subjects without the required support. Additional problems include:

- lack of appropriate IT skills by students (and staff)
- inadequate access to the web from some clinical sites
- for academics, a large time commitment monitoring online discussions and providing individualized feedback, which is expected promptly and at all hours of the day and evening (including weekends).

A related issue is that of learning styles. The profiling exercise described in *Chapter 2* made some attempts to understand practitioners' preferred learning styles. These were many and varied, but many of those in senior positions in the cancer and palliative care workforce who were profiled showed a strong activist persuasion. In education, the mode of learning is often as important as the content, and ensuring a match of preferred learning style with delivery method is paramount for success. Work-based learning may be a better match than e-learning for activist learners; this is something that needs to be taken into consideration, despite the challenge that it will present to more traditional education providers.

Another major factor that will impact on educational delivery and support is the rapid increase in the numbers of managed clinical networks (MCNs) in the NHS. Professional boundaries are being eroded and roles are changing at a phenomenal rate to keep pace with changes and technological developments in the healthcare environment.

'A shift is required towards a health service where the competence, training and facilities to provide a service are more important than professional labels. MCNs offer a way of facilitating that change, and the direct involvement of patients should help to speed the shift that has already started in the public's attitude.'
(Baker, 2002)

Education and CPD providers need to interact with the networks and work in partnership with them to ensure that they remain at the forefront of cancer and palliative care.

Universities and other providers of education may face the biggest challenge of all. As education moves back to the workplace, with an emphasis on showing how it contributes to specific knowledge and skills to undertake specific roles, a number of theoretical masters' degrees will become redundant. The challenge for educators is to match provision to clinical need and ensure that the value and worth of their provision can be demonstrated. Educators may wish to advise potential students which knowledge and skills framework (KSF) dimensions are met from their learning and experience, as practitioners in the NHS (with the exception of doctors, dentists and pharmacists) build learning plans around their KSF outlines. The requirement to work in close partnership with clinical colleagues and to break down the walls that exist between higher education institutions and clinical practice has never been greater.

Evaluating the effectiveness of CPD

The need for CPD is now well established; however, there is still some question over how best to provide CPD and how to measure its effectiveness. There is an underlying belief that undertaking regular and relevant CPD will help to maintain and improve standards, but there is little empirical evidence to support this view.

Henwood (2003) undertook an extended study of CPD in radiography to establish which factors contributed to its effectiveness. The framework has subsequently been tested through a seminar programme in Macmillan Cancer Relief; this showed that the framework is transferable to nursing (the target audience for the study) and is useful in helping individuals and departments to reflect on CPD activity and identify the drivers and barriers to effective CPD.

The final section of this chapter will briefly describe that framework to allow readers to consider effectiveness issues in a new way.

Central to Henwood's (2003) framework (*Figure 7.2*) is the individual component, i.e. his/her attitude towards development, motivation and previous experience of CPD. This is often left out of studies on CPD effectiveness, many of which focus on the degree of funding or time off granted to undertake CPD. Surrounding the individual is 'Facilitation', which looks at the broader aspects of support, enabling CPD to take place.

This comprises both individual facilitation – being prepared to fund his/her own activities and study in his/her own time – and employer support. Surrounding 'Facilitation' is the concept of 'External Influences', which includes mandates, for example, and more recently the necessity to have a KSF outline and associated learning plan for nurses and AHPs within the NHS. The three main elements are interlinked and interdependent, making the framework complex but realistic. Each element has a relatively static component, which is unlikely to change in the short term and which, with appropriate reflection, can be subjectively quantified by either an individual or a manager on behalf of a department. In addition, each element has a more dynamic component, which can change more easily over time and which moves the individual on to the next stage of the process.

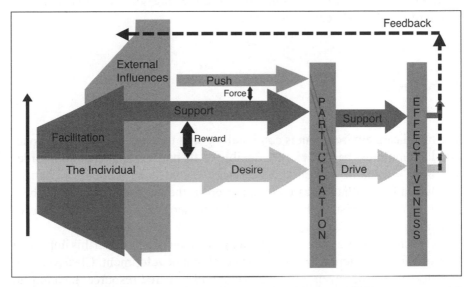

Figure 7.2: Henwood's continuous professional development (CPD) process model

If there is sufficient consistency within the three components (and all three working together give added value/impact) then the individual is likely to move onto 'Participation' in CPD (using the broad definition of CPD, and not restricting it to attendance-based activities offsite). If, and only if, the components of the individual and 'Facilitation' extend beyond 'Participation', it is likely that there will be some 'Effectiveness' evident from that activity. 'Participation' alone is insufficient to generate change. A challenge to education providers would be how to support this phase in practice: what support should be offered following formal CPD activities to help participants take learning back into the workplace and to implement changes over time?

The framework is itself dynamic (merely a snapshot of any one point in time) and after each CPD activity the individual re-enters a new CPD phase and should re-examine the individual components in light of the latest activities. By subjectively measuring and quantifying the scope of each component, the framework allows an individual to assess the effectiveness of his/her own CPD activity and to identify where improvements can be made.

The Henwood CPD process model offers a genuinely holistic approach to measuring the impact of CPD. Both participants and providers of CPD opportunities need to consider the potential impact on practice. The recently published *Health Professions Council: Standards for CPD* (Health Professions Council, 2005) requires AHPs to demonstrate how their CPD has benefited the service and patients. With the imperative, outlined previously, of making the patient the epicentre of palliative care services, this should be standard for all healthcare practitioners.

Conclusion

The healthcare environment is continually going through change. Any model of education must be sufficiently flexible to respond to that change in order to ensure a valuable and effective service. A significant number of changes that will affect palliative care are expected in the next few years, and there are a number of issues that could, if taken seriously, change the face of education.

This chapter has explored the challenges facing education in this important area of care and offered a model of professional development. Clearly, as the workforce becomes even more important and a scarce resource, meaningful development minimizing the time away from the workplace will be of paramount importance. We hope that this chapter provokes some thinking about what that future might look like.

References

Baker C (2002) NHS Scotland. *What are Managed Clinical Networks?* Hayward Medical Communications, Newmarket. Available at: http://www.Pfizer.co.uk/pdf/MCN%208pp. pdf (accessed 26.04.06)

Buchan J, Seccombe I (2003) *More Nurses, Working Differently? A review of the UK nursing labour market in 2002*. Royal College of Nursing, London

Crisp N (2005) *Commissioning a Patient-Led NHS*. Gateway Ref. No: 5312. Department of Health, London

Davies E, Higginson J (2004) *The Solid Facts: Palliative Care*. WHO Regional Office for Europe, Copenhagen, Denmark

Delva MD, Kirby JR, Knapper CK, Birtwhistle RV (2002) Postal survey of approaches to learning among Ontario physicians: implications for continuing medical education. *BMJ* **325**(7374): 1218

Department of Health (1999) *Making a Difference: Strengthening the nursing, midwifery and health visiting contribution to health and healthcare*. The Stationery Office, London

Department of Health (2000) *The NHS Plan: A plan for investment, a plan for reform*. HMSO, London

Department of Health (2001) *A Health Service of all the Talents: Developing the NHS workforce. Results of consultation*. DH, London

Department of Health (2004a) *Agenda for Change: What will it mean for you? A guide for staff*. Available at: http://www.dh.gov.uk/assetRoot/04/09/08/59/04090859.pdf (accessed 28.03.06)

Department of Health (2004b) *The NHS Knowledge and Skills Framework and the Development Review Process*. Chapter One – An introduction to the NHS Knowledge and Skills Framework and its use in career and pay progression. Available at:

http://www.dh.gov.uk/PublicationsAndStatistics/Publications/PublicationsPolicyAndGuidan ce/PublicationsPolicyAndGuidanceArticle/fs/en?CONTENT_ID=4090843&chk=dyrb/a (accessed 28.03.06)

Department of Health (2005) *National Service Framework for Long-Term Conditions*. DH, London

Department of Health (2006) *Your Health, Your Care, Your Say*. Research report. DH, London

Fordham S, Dowrick C, May C (1998) Palliative medicine: is it really specialist territory? *J R Soc Med* **91**(11): 568–72

Health Professions Council (2005) *Health Professions Council: Standards for Continuing Professional Development*. HPC, London

Henwood SM (2003) Continuing professional development in diagnostic radiography: a grounded theory study. PhD thesis, South Bank University, London

Kendall L (2001) *The Future Patient*. Institute of Public Policy Research, London

King's Fund (2002) *The Future of the NHS: A framework for debate*. King's Fund, London

Murray SA, Grant E, Grant A, Kendall M (2003) Dying from cancer in developed and developing countries: lessons from two qualitative interview studies of patients and their carers. *BMJ* **326**(7385): 368

National Death Alliance (2005) A group of academics who have come together to tackle taboos around death in UK society – unpublished as yet

Wanless D (2002) *Securing our Future Health: Taking a long-term view*. Final report. Available at: http://www.hm-treasury.gov.uk/Consultations_and_Legislation/wanless/ consult_wanless_final.cfm (last accessed 26.04.06)

Woods KJ (2002) Health policy and the NHS in the UK 1997-2002. In: Adams J, Robinson P (eds) *Devolution in Practice: Public policy differences within the UK*. Institute of Public Policy Research, London

The last word

Liz Searle

This book has described a journey of learning, a process for supporting role transition. For the authors the process of supporting work-based learning is being lost, partly due to the reduction in the numbers of qualified staff in practice and, to some extent, the shift of nursing courses to an academic base. Universities clearly need to provide a degree of academic rigour, but the challenge of ensuring that a student practitioner is competent to practise still stretches assessment strategists and regulators.

We are approaching a time when the number of people entering the caring profession will be considerably reduced. Initiatives such as the skills escalator, and to some extent Agenda for Change, attempt to enable staff to travel up the professional ladder to the top. If this is to be successful, then support for role transition will be vital.

This book has shown how learning needs can be identified, how education programmes can be developed in response to meeting these needs, and how evaluation can be used to further develop these programmes. Time and financial constraints may present challenges to this approach. However, we would argue that we cannot afford not to ensure adequate support for role transition and competence. Much of this work was made possible by Macmillan Cancer Relief, who provided the funds, and by the forward thinking of the partner universities who hosted the education units. Without support from both organizations, the vast amount of learning about work-based processes by the education team and the new learning opportunities available to healthcare professionals would not have been possible.

While this book concentrates on the process and outcomes of education, there was another significant piece of organizational learning that was not included in the book but deserves mention. This unique way of working as a virtual institute enabled a group of diverse educators based in different geographical locations to become a successful team under the Macmillan National Institute of Education. The experience and knowledge gained from it will stay with all those involved in bringing the programme to fruition.

The future for healthcare education is challenging. Managing the cost and time of the professional workforce will continue to be a highly pressured activity for managers. We encourage all organizations and managers within them to reflect on how they support learning and role transition – if for no other reason than to support, recruit and retain the best practitioners. For this to be successful, a strong partnership between practitioners, managers and educators will be required.

We hope that by sharing our experiences and knowledge gained along this journey, we have shown how a complex partnership can achieve success.

Appendix I

Macmillan Educational Profiling: User Guide

Introduction

This guide has been prepared for those Macmillan lecturers or other educational facilitators who are preparing to profile Macmillan postholders using the Macmillan Educational Profiling Tool. To fully prepare the educator, the user guide should be read in conjunction with three other key documents held in the Macmillan Education Units (MEUs):

- *Evaluation of Profiling* (Macmillan Cancer Relief, 2001)
- *Information for Postholders and Managers to Support the Profiling Process* (Macmillan National Institute of Education [MNIE], 2004)
- *The Learning Styles Questionnaire* (Honey and Mumford, 2000)

A specialist practitioner is a person who demonstrates higher levels of clinical decision making and can monitor and improve standards of care through supervision of practice, clinical audit, developing and leading practice and teaching and supporting professional colleagues (UKCC, 2002).

Specialist posts funded by Macmillan Cancer Relief include clinical nurse specialists (CNSs), specialist occupational therapists, physiotherapists, dieticians, social workers and information radiographers who work in the field of cancer and palliative care. Specialist appointments are generally at first degree level, with many Macmillan postholders now completing higher degrees. However, the changing nature of cancer and palliative care services, and the evolving of the specialist role within a changing NHS, necessitates a clear framework for continued professional development within cancer and palliative care to meet service needs detailed in policy documents such as *Agenda for Change* (DH, 1999), *The NHS Cancer Plan* (DH, 2000) and *A Health Service of all the Talents* (DH, 2001).

The educational profiling exercise has been developed to facilitate the process of identifying the learning and development needs of Macmillan postholders. The profiling tool offers a framework for exploring the components of the specialist role as it relates to the service, job description and operational policy of the individual postholder. A key outcome of the profile is an action plan developed in partnership with the postholder, their manager and Macmillan Cancer Relief, which provides a description of the learning needs and actions to be undertaken to meet those needs for the individual concerned.

Where possible, Macmillan Cancer Relief, in partnership with the employing Trust, will support the meeting of the identified education and development needs agreed in the action plan by the provision of education grants, the support of the professional resources service and the provision of Macmillan courses, seminars and conferences. Trust contributions to the education and development of a Macmillan postholder may include a financial contribution to development costs, travel expenses or protected time. An action plan countersigned by the postholder's manager is now requested as evidence towards an application for a Macmillan grant, although the day when each application is accompanied by a signed action plan still seems far away!

The aim of educational profiling is:

To enable Macmillan postholders to identify and meet their learning and development needs within the context of their specialist practitioner role.

Objectives

- To increase awareness of the components of the role of the specialist practitioner.
- To provide individualised educational facilitation to complement existing organisational appraisal schemes.
- To facilitate personal reflection on the role of the postholder and their associated learning and development needs.
- To support postholders through role transition from a generalist to a specialist practitioner post.

- To inform Macmillan Cancer Relief of the learning and development needs of specialist practitioners in order to develop appropriate education provision.
- To work in partnership with health service managers to facilitate the continuing professional development of postholders.
- To provide equitable educational facilitation to Macmillan specialist practitioners across the UK.
- To provide evidence for the award of a Macmillan Education Grant.

Data protection, confidentiality and the profiling record

The record of the profiling meeting itself (the action plan) remains a confidential document, although there is a clear expectation that the action plan is shared with managers and colleagues. Profiling elicits personal information, which postholders may, or may not, want recording. Disclosures within a profiling meeting should be held in strictest confidence.

The action plan should be held in the personal file of the postholder, which should be kept in a locked cabinet. The electronic copy should be password protected. The MEU administrator will have a system for ensuring that confidentiality is maintained.

In order to comply with the Data Protection Act (1998), postholders who request profiling will be asked to sign a consent form (*Appendix 1a*), which details what happens to their personal data. The consent form is crucial to protect the rights of the postholder and Macmillan Cancer Relief.

Outcomes of profiling

An evaluation conducted from the perspective of 235 Macmillan CNSs who had been profiled between 1999 and 2000 (Macmillan Cancer Relief, 2001) captured a number of key outcomes related to the profiling process. These included:

- Identification of learning and development needs
- Facilitation of meeting learning and development needs
- Expansion of awareness of specialist role components and activity
- Enabling of increased focus and direction

- Increased confidence
- Positive impact on patient care
- Increased perception of support and feeling valued.

The Macmillan CNSs surveyed overwhelmingly found the profiling exercise useful, and many commented on the benefits of an external facilitator. The survey provided rich data on the usefulness of profiling, although a minority reported some difficulties, which generally related to working in unsupportive organisations. On the basis of this evaluation, profiling was extended to other Macmillan postholders in 2001 (excluding medics).

The Profiling Tool

Although profiling is a structured process utilising the profiling tool, the Macmillan lecturers are very aware that personal style and preferences influence the approach taken in the profiling meeting. The current version of the tool has been developed through experience, discussion and consultation. Some parts of the original tool have been removed, for example, the profiling components developed from the higher level practice descriptors (UKCC, 2002) and a competency rating scale. These are shown in *Appendixes 1b* and *1c*, and may be used to inform your discussion with the postholder.

The profiling tool is reprinted below, with cues to guide questioning or discussion. These cues have been generated from a review of documents from the nursing and allied healthcare professions, from cancer/palliative care policy documents and from general NHS policy documents.

Context of the post

This could include:

- Rationale for post
- In or out of funding, adopted
- Lone postholder or part of team
- New or replacement post
- Admin support
- Multidisciplinary team profile
- Referral routes

- Client group
- Brief outline of remit within organisation
- Brief review of remit in terms of job description and operational policy documents

Education and learning history

This could include:

- Brief review of CV to reflect on experience of education and continuing professional development since qualifying
- Completion of learning styles exercise and scores
- Ways of developing learning styles (reference to *The Learning Styles Questionnaire* booklet)

Work history

This could include:

- Brief review of CV to discuss their path to their current role
- Transferable skills/what the postholder brought to their current post
- Becoming aware of the wider issues in cancer and palliative care
- Managing a caseload/managerial experiences.

Components of the specialist role

Providing effective healthcare

This could include how the postholder:

- Analyses and reflects on own practice
- Is effective as an independent practitioner
- Has advanced decision making skills
- Uses self to influence practice

- Utilises effective communication skills
- Manages complex care episodes
- Demonstrates user-focused practice
- Is effective within multidisciplinary team
- Positively impacts on other teams
- Develops effective information strategies
- Demonstrates sound rationale for clinical interventions
- Empowers non-specialist staff
- Balances caseload with other components of role
- Works effectively across professional and organisational boundaries.

Developing self and others

This could include how the postholder:

- Demonstrates continuing professional development through work-based learning and other mechanisms
- Takes opportunities to develop practice through teaching and educational activities
- Demonstrates user involvement in educational activities
- Demonstrates self-awareness about the impact of their own development on colleagues and the service.

Quality, evaluation and research

This could include how the postholder:

- Demonstrates quality improvement initiatives
- Improves health outcomes of client group
- Demonstrates ability to work with information systems, data handling, and IT
- Audits/evaluates care and services
- Works within the context of clinical and cost effectiveness
- Demonstrates user involvement in quality improvement, evaluation and research
- Is able to access research evidence
- Is able to analyse/utilise/disseminate research evidence
- Participates in research initiatives.

Leading and developing practice

This could include how the postholder:

- Demonstrates resource and people management
- Demonstrates user involvement in service and strategic development
- Works strategically in the context of national policy and local service development
- Utilises and influences the political agenda
- Utilises leadership and consultancy skills
- Networks locally, regionally and nationally
- Generates innovative work practices/extended roles
- Implements local and national standards
- Manages change
- Demonstrates project management skills.

Current strengths

This could include:

- Summarising good work in one or more of the role components
- Personal strengths
- Elements of the post the postholder finds satisfying and enjoyable
- Strengths of the overall service.

Learning and development needs

This could include:

- Gaps in specialist knowledge or skills
- Things to enable them to fulfil job requirements
- Their personal goals in the workplace
- Consolidation of learning
- Implementation of learning into practice
- Identification of priorities
- Short-term and long-term goals.

Opportunities and constraints to meeting needs

Opportunities may include:

- Formal course/study days
- Macmillan course/seminars
- Workplace projects or activities
- Mentorship/clinical supervision systems
- Restructuring within organisation
- Secondments or time in other departments or services
- Supportive organisation/manager.

    Constraints may include:

- Personal pressures on postholder
- Release from service
- Development of other team members
- Too many development needs! – further prioritisation
- Unsupportive organisation/manager
- Uncertainty due to organisational restructuring.

Proposed ways of meeting needs/draft action plan

The proposed ways of meeting learning and development needs can be recorded straight onto the action plan, considering the priorities and opportunities available.

Issues to consider at future meetings

This considers what the postholder might like to reflect on one year down the line.

The profiling process

Educational profiling may be of benefit to Macmillan postholders at any stage of their careers. For new Macmillan postholders, a structured programme is recommended for the first year in post, which includes organisational induction (0–3 months), attendance on '*Setting Out*' (between 4 and 9 months in post), followed by educational profiling.

The postholder is responsible for contacting the MEU to arrange the profiling meeting. A review is offered about 12 months after the initial profile to enable postholders to revisit and review their action plans. The MEU administrator will have a system in place for offering reviews.

Macmillan postholders will hear about profiling from a variety of sources including: service development managers, *Setting Out*, team members and other colleagues who have been profiled, discussion at Macmillan seminars or direct contact with the MEU.

Postholders are informed in the *Information for Postholders and Managers to Support the Profiling Process* (MNIE, 2004) that:

- Profiling is confidential
- The meeting takes approximately one and a half hours
- The meeting takes place at the MEU, or at a mutually acceptable location
- A quiet, undisturbed setting is necessary
- Telephone appointments or video conferencing may be alternatives if differences are insurmountable
- There is an expectation that the draft action plan is discussed, reviewed and agreed with the manager of the postholder.

Once the profiling appointment is made, the MEU administrator will:

- Send a letter confirming date, time and meeting venue
- The letter should request CV, operational policy and job description documentation to be sent to the MEU before the meeting
- Send the booklet *Information for Postholders and Managers*
- Send the Learning Styles Questionnaire and *Using Your Learning Styles* booklet
- Inform the postholder's manager by letter about the profiling appointment, and enclose the profiling information. The manager will be invited in the letter to contact or meet the Macmillan lecturer for further information or discussion

Before the profiling meeting, the Macmillan lecturer/educational facilitator will review the documentation sent by the postholder.

Preparation by the Macmillan postholder

- Discuss request for profiling with manager
- Send CV, job description, operational policy and completed profiling tool to the Macmillan lecturer in advance of the meeting
- Review above documents
- Complete the Learning Styles Questionnaire

The role of the manager

The input of the manager varies enormously from service to service. The rule of thumb is to invite discussion and contact, and encourage the postholder to keep the manager well informed.

Practical tips

- Occasionally, the profile tool has to be abandoned to address the needs of postholders with very specific difficulties.
- For managers meetings, take or send MNIE info you think will be useful, eg. programme leaflets and your card.
- Be clear about the differences between appraisal and profiling – managers are likely to raise this!
- Discuss with the administrator the format/content of letters that go out on your behalf. You may want to modify the core letters.

Quality monitoring

The profiling process is subject to the *Profiling Standard (Appendix 1d)*, for which there is a *Profiling Audit Tool*, which is used to check that the standard is being met. The MEU team will decide on audit processes, but the administrator completes a *Profiling Checklist*, which sits in the front of each postholder's file. Completion of this checklist by the administrator makes the audit process straightforward.

Appendix 1a

Use and Storage of Personal and Profiling Data

Consent form

I have asked to be profiled and understand that this will produce personal and profile data about me that the Macmillan Education Unit (MEU) doing my profile will hold on my behalf in both paper and electronic format.

When I am profiled I understand that my personal and profile data will be recorded onto forms by a MEU lecturer and that Macmillan Cancer Relief and the MEUs will use this information for two purposes:

1. To facilitate me in developing my action plan
2. To audit the profiling process and the profiling tool.

I understand that in order for Macmillan Cancer Relief to meet both these purposes, some or all of the other MEUs at the Universities of Central England, Wales, Leeds, Plymouth and Glasgow and Macmillan Cancer Relief's Department of Education, Development and Support, may need to review my profile. If my action plan is to be seen by MEU lecturers other than at the unit creating my action plan or by the Department of Education, Development and Support, I understand that my personal details will be removed to protect my confidentiality and privacy.

I understand that all my data will be held securely by the MEUs and Macmillan Cancer Relief and that I can update my data by contacting the MEU lecturer who initially profiled me.

If Macmillan Cancer Relief or the MEUs wish to use my profile data for purposes of research, or to transfer my data to a third party, I understand that they will contact me to explain about the project and to ask for written consent, to which I am free to say either 'yes' or 'no'.

I understand that Macmillan Cancer Relief and the MEUs will hold all my data for a long period of time for the legitimate purpose of research, evaluating services and developing education programmes. I understand that if I do not wish my data to be held I need to tell my MEU lecturer now, before the profiling starts.

I consent to Macmillan Cancer Relief and the MEUs storing and using my data.

Name of Postholder   Date   Signature

_____   _____   _____

Name of MEU lecturer   Date   Signature

_____   _____   _____

Appendix 1b

Components of Specialist Practice developed from the Higher Level Practice Descriptors (UKCC, 2002)

- **The use of self in practice**
  Demonstrates an awareness of self and is able to develop self as a positive influencing factor in practice. Is able to critically analyse and reflect on practice, work within boundaries, and is able to identify and utilise appropriate support structures, eg. clinical supervision

- **Leading and developing practice**
  Challenges professional and organisational boundaries in the interest of patients, and to improve health outcomes. Is able to develop and apply strategies to learn effectively from others. Demonstrates ability to work collaboratively across the disciplines and, where appropriate, takes the lead in developing documentation, standards, policies and clinical guidelines. Networks locally, regionally and nationally to develop collaborative working with other healthcare professionals. Acts as a resource for staff, patients and carers.

- **Providing effective health care (direct and indirect services)**
  Uses a confident and assertive approach, demonstrates ability to identify and manage complex care episodes. Is able to lead and empower other healthcare professionals using appropriate referral and discharge policies. Delegates to other professionals, utilises resources effectively, and is able to work within a multidisciplinary team setting.

- **Evaluation and research**
  Seeks opportunities to apply new knowledge and promotes the use of evidence-based practice. Is able to access and utilise research material and seeks opportunities to broaden and deepen nursing knowledge. Always chooses interventions based on sound rationale. Is aware of the importance of continually auditing and evaluating own and others'

practice using a broad range of valid and reliable methods. Is able to utilise the results of audit to inform and improve practice.

- **Develop self and others**
  Continues to address his/her own personal and professional development needs. Develops and uses appropriate strategies and opportunities to share knowledge and expertise with other professionals, patients and carers. Continually strives to improve practice through teaching and educational activities.

- **Improving quality and health outcomes**
  Operates efficiently and effectively within a culture of clinical and cost effectiveness (clinical governance). Is able to utilise information systems and has an understanding of how information technology can contribute to clinical practice. Demonstrates decision-making skills and ability to balance the conflicting components of the role. Takes the lead in the implementation of health and social policy and utilises a variety of information systems. Seeks opportunities to influence health policy locally, regionally and nationally. Actively promotes the service.

- **Working across professional and organisational boundaries**
  Demonstrates ability to work flexibly across professional boundaries. Is aware of the potential macro and micro issues that can influence team dynamics. Is able to manage group and organisational relationships in a way that supports intended outcomes.

- **Innovation and changing practice**
  Is proactive in managing and promoting change to improve practice and health outcomes. Takes the lead in the implementation of local and national standards as appropriate. Is able to contribute to the development of his/her area of practice, and think laterally about his/her own and others' practice in order to generate new solutions to meet the needs of patients and carers.

Appendix 1c

Competency Rating Scale

You might want to invite the postholder to rate him/herself on a scale of 0–5 with regard to either the components or his/her competency within each component. Scores could be interpreted as follows:

Components		Competencies	
0	I have yet to consider this aspect of the role	0	No opportunity to apply
1	There is some difficulty in interpreting this aspect of my role	1	Aware
2	I am aware of this aspect but lack confidence/opportunity	2	Aware and demonstrates application
3	Familiar with this aspect	3	Demonstrates competence
4	Recognises and uses this aspect of the role	4	Confident and competent
5	Fully confident	5	Expert, fully integrated

Appendix 1d

MNIE Profiling Standard

Standard Statement: All Macmillan postholders (excluding medics) will be offered educational profiling in order to facilitate their learning and development.

S = Standard statement for MEU structure
P = Standard statements for MEU processes
O = Standard statements for MEU outcomes

S1   Regional MEU checklist completed

P1   MEU will send pre-meeting information to postholder and manager at least 3 weeks before profiling meeting
P2   MEU lecturer will make contact with the postholder's manager prior to profiling
P3   MEU will request copies of postholder's CV, operational policy, job description and completed profiling tool to arrive before the profiling meeting
P4   Lecturer and postholder will review above documents before profiling meeting
P5   Lecturer will discuss consent and keep signed consent form
P6   Profiling tool will be used as a framework for discussion
P7   Draft action plan sent to postholder
P8   MEU will receive signed action plan (signed by postholder and manager)
P9   Non-receipt of action plan followed up by MEU
P10 Review (about 12 months after profiling) will be offered to postholder
P11 Action plans will be stored in accordance with the Data Protection Act

---

O1   All Macmillan postholders (excluding medics) will be offered educational profiling
O2   MEUs will have signed consent forms for all those postholders who have been profiled
O3   All Macmillan postholders will have a signed action plan following the profiling exercise
O4   Applications for Macmillan Cancer Relief education grants from postholders who have been profiled will be accompanied by their action plan

---

References

Department of Health (1999) *Agenda for Change: Modernising the NHS pay system.* DH, London

Department of Health (2000) *The NHS Cancer Plan: A plan for investment, a plan for reform.* DH, London

Department of Health (2001) *A Health Service of All the Talents: Developing the NHS workforce – consultation document on the review of workforce planning – results of consultation.* DH, London

Honey P, Mumford A (2000) *The Learning Styles Questionnaire: 80-item version.* Peter Honey Publications, Maidenhead

Macmillan Cancer Relief (2001) *Evaluation of Profiling.* Unpublished internal report

Macmillan National Institute of Education (2004) *Information for Postholders and Managers to Support the Profiling Process.* Booklet produced by MNIE

UKCC (2002) *Report of the Higher Level of Practice Pilot and Project.* UKCC, London

Appendix 2: Key policy documents that informed the profiling review

- Higher level practice descriptors (UKCC, 1999)
- Working Together, Learning together: A framework for lifelong learning for the NHS (DH, 2001)
- Meeting the Challenge: A strategy for the allied health professions (DH, 2000)
- Ten Key Roles for Allied Health Professionals (DH, 2003)
- A Framework for Nurses Working in Specialist Palliative Care (RCN, 2002)
- Supportive and Palliative Care for People with Cancer (draft) (NICE, 2003)
- A Health Service of All the Talents: Developing the NHS workforce – results of consultation (DH, 2001)
- Liberating the Talents: Helping primary care trusts and nurses to deliver the NHS Plan (DH, 2002)
- *Agenda for Change* (DH, 2003)
- The NHS Knowledge and Skills Framework (NHS KSF) and Development Review Guidance: working draft (DH, 2003)
- Macmillan Service Review Template (Macmillan Cancer Relief)
- Making a Difference: Strengthening the nursing, midwifery and health visiting contribution to health and healthcare (DH, 1999)
- Developing, Delivering and Evaluating Cancer Nursing Services: Building the evidence base (Richardson *et al*, 2002)
- Developing Key Roles for Nurses and Midwives – A guide for managers (DH, 2002)

References

Department of Health (1999) *Making a Difference: Strengthening the nursing, midwifery and health visiting contribution to health and healthcare.* DH, London

Department of Health (2000) *Meeting the Challenge: A strategy for the allied health professions.* DH, London

Department of Health (2001a) *Working Together, Learning together: A framework for lifelong learning for the NHS.* HMSO, London

Department of Health (2001b) *A Health Service of All the Talents: Developing the NHS workforce – consultation document on the review of workforce planning – results of consultation.* DH, London

Department of Health (2002a) *Liberating the Talents: Helping primary care trusts and nurses to deliver the NHS Plan.* DH, London

Department of Health (2002b) *Developing Key Roles for Nurses and Midwives – A guide for managers.* DH, London

Department of Health (2003a) *Ten Key Roles for Allied Health Professionals.* DH, London

Department of Health (2003b) *Agenda for Change.* DH, London

Department of Health (2003c) *The NHS Knowledge and Skills Framework (NHS KSF) and Development Review Guidance: working draft.* DH, London

National Institute for Health and Clinical Excellence (NICE) (2003) *Supportive and Palliative Care for People with Cancer* (draft). NICE, London

Royal College of Nursing (2002) *A Framework for Nurses Working in Specialist Palliative Care.* RCN, London

Richardson A, Miller M, Potter H (2002) *Developing, Delivering and Evaluating Cancer Nursing Services: Building the evidence base.* Kings College, London

UKCC (1999) *A Higher Level of Practice. Report of the consultation on the UKCC's proposal for a revised regulatory framework for post-registration clinical practice.* UKCC, London

Index

M

Macmillan Education Units
  (MEUs) 18, 19, 20, 21
  profiling 131, 139
Macmillan Educational Profiling
  99, 131–41
  evaluation 22–6, 27, 136
  lecturer perspective 27
  outcome delivery 20–2
  patient care impact 26–7
  review 22–4, 28, 29–32
  standard 19, 147
  tool 18–20
Macmillan Management
  Fellowship 89–90
Macmillan Mentorship Training
  Programme (MMTP) 36, 41,
  42–7
  action learning 44, 45–6, 50–1
  design 48
  development 43
  evaluation 48–51
  experiential learning 44, 45–6
  mentorship relationship 44–5
  method 48
  outcome achievement 49–51
  rationale 42–3
  structure 43–7
  workshop 43–4
Macmillan National Institute of
  Education (MNIE) 11
  conference 95–7
  development climate 23
  educational development/
  support 115
  educational seminars 101
  evaluation of activities 24
  learning climate 23
  lecturers 105
    action learning facilitation
    47

appointments 21
  masterclasses 108–9, 110
management fellowship
  89–90
masterclass programme 106–
  11
practice-based facilitator
  training 72
professional workforce 104
research fellowship/
  scholarship 90
service development
  managers 48, 49, 105
'setting out' 97–100
teaching fellowship 90
virtual institute 129
Macmillan nurse specialist roles
  13
  profiling tool pilot 16–18
Macmillan Role Development
  Programme (MRDP) 67–73
  assessment 70–1
  evaluation 72
  support 71–2
  work-based learning 77–8
Macmillan Teaching Fellowship
  90
managed clinical networks
  (MCNs) 123–4
management, specialist practice
  70
masterclass programme 106–11
  content 108
  delivery 108–9
  evaluation 109–10
mentor 39
  definition 36
mentoring relationship 39–40,
  44–5
  classical/contracted 41
  phases 44–5
mentorship 8, 35–51

clinical nurse specialists   14
development planning   116
see also clinical nurse
specialists (CNS); nurse
practitioner
pre-registration nursing   2–4
prior occupational socialisation
65
problem-based learning   6
professional boundaries   123–4
working across   145
professional development   116
professional growth   40
professional roles   5
profiling/profiling tools   99,
131–41
action plans   132, 133
added value   32
aims   132–3
components/competencies
14–16
confidentiality   133
consent forms   133, 142–3
context of post   134–5
cost-effectiveness   32
critical discussion   23
current strengths   137
data protection   133
data use/storage   142–3
design   13–16
development   12–18
needs   137–8
difficulties   27
education history   135
evaluation   22–6, 27, 136
instrument   13–22
leading   137
learning
history   135
needs   137–8
manager role   140
meeting   139

MNIE standard   147
modified   30–1
objectives   132–3
outcomes   133–4
delivery   20–2
patient care impact   26–7
piloting   16–18
policy documents for review
149
practice development   137
principles   12
process   139–40
quality   136
monitoring   141
records   133
research   136
review   22–4, 28, 29–32
rolling out   18–20
specialist role components
30–1
standard   19, 147
structured programme   139
tool   18–20
user guide   131–41
values   12
work history   135
prognosis, end-of-life care   119
Project 2000   3, 8
provider roles   119–20

Q

quality improvement   145
questionnaires, mentorship   48,
49–51

R

reflective practitioner model   41–2
reflective processes   45
regressive progression   65–6
research   144–5